D1633616

Walking
Glencoe, Lochaber and the Great Glen

Clan Walk Guides

Walking
Glencoe, Lochaber
and the Great Glen

Mary Welsh
and
Christine Isherwood

First published by Clan Books, 2006

ISBN 1 873597 22 3
Text and Illustrations
© Mary Welsh
and
Christine Isherwood
2006

The authors wish to express their gratitude to Jennifer Outhwaite
for her help in preparing this volume.

Clan Books
Clandon House
The Cross, Doune
Perthshire
FK16 6BE

Printed and bound in Great Britain by
St. Edmundsbury Press, Bury St. Edmunds, Suffolk

Authors' Note

Please remember on all these walks:

Wear suitable clothes and take adequate waterproofs.

Walk in strong footwear; walking boots are advisable.

Carry the relevant map and know how to use it.

Take extra food and drink as emergency rations.

Carry a whistle; remember six long blasts repeated at one minute intervals is the distress signal.

Do not walk alone, and tell someone where you are going.

If mist descends, return.

Keep all dogs under strict control. Observe all 'No Dogs' notices—they are there for very good reasons.

Readers are advised that while the authors have taken every effort to ensure the accuracy of this guidebook, changes can occur after publication. You should check locally on transport, accommodation, etc. The publisher would welcome notes of any changes. Neither the publisher nor the authors can accept responsibility for errors, omissions or any loss or injury.

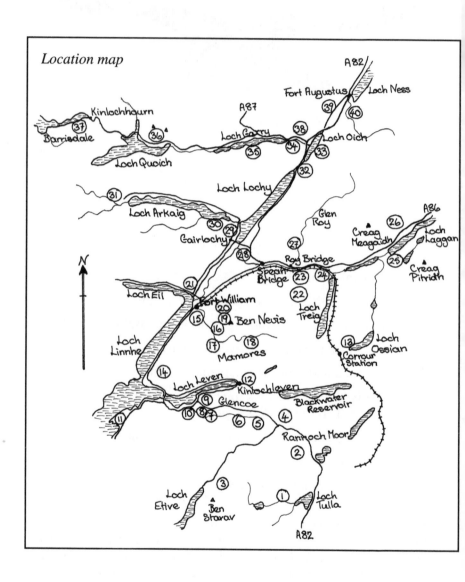

Location map

Contents

Contents continued page 6

1

Loch Dochard

Park in Victoria Bridge car park, grid ref. 271418. A notice board at the north end of the car park gives local information, weather forecasts, and preferred routes during the stalking season, from mid-August to mid-October. To access this, leave the A82 at Bridge of Orchy, and take the minor road, west, beside the Bridge of Orchy Hotel, signposted 'Inveroran and Forest Lodge'. This road runs through the splendid Caledonian pinewood, the Coille Doire Darach, which stretches up the hill from the southern shores of Loch Tulla. About ¾ mile beyond the wood is the Inveroran Hotel, then the road crosses the Allt Tolaghan by a stone bridge and, a few hundred yards further on, a track on the left leads to the car park.

Inveroran Inn is an old drovers' inn, dating from 1707. It is strategically sited on both the drove road over Rannoch Moor,

Loch Tulla

and Major Caulfeild's military road, built in the early 1750s, and now used by the West Highland Way. It is a good place to quench your thirst at the end of this long walk.

Duncan Ban Macintyre is one of the most famous Gaelic poets. Born in 1724 at Druimliart, he spent most of his life in the area, later becoming a stalker and living at Ais an t-Sidhean in Gleann Chonoghlais behind Beinn Dorain. His poems mostly dealt with mountains, deer and the chase.

Walk 1

1 Leave the car park by the entrance and turn left on the metalled road, to cross Victoria Bridge over the Abhainn Shira. Go on to the road end at the entrances to the Blackmount Estate and Forest Lodge. Turn left on to a vehicle track, with a Scottish Rights of Way Society signpost to Loch Etive. This leads through a small wood of mature Scots pines to a gate (if the gate is locked, walkers can wind round the end of the short fence). The track follows the meanders of the Abhainn Shira, to reach a small, green, corrugated-iron hut, a former schoolhouse for the children of Clashgour and surrounding scattered settlements. It is now the hut of the Glasgow University Mountaineering Club. Ignore a well-made stalkers' path to the right and go on along the track, which crosses the Allt Toaig on a flat wooden bridge.

2 Carry on along the public footpath, signposted Loch Etive, which leaves the track to the left and follows the riverbank. This small path is well-defined and mostly dry and grassy. There are a few small burns to cross, some on wooden bridges. The river on the left is delightful, its peaty waters sometimes flowing calmly, sometimes over rapids, and the pebble banks and shoals are ideal places to spot a dipper. Ahead are the mountains between this Glen

8

and Glen Etive. These are Beinn nan Aighenan, Glas Bheinn Mhor and Stob Coir an Albannaich, all notable for their huge slabs of granite, which when wet, glisten in the sunshine.

3 After a mile, the path meets another track coming down from Clashgour Farm to the Abhainn Shira. Cross the Allt Ghabhar on a substantial wooden bridge, built in 2001 by the Royal Engineers for the Blackmount Partnership. Follow the bank of this tributary for a few yards, and go round the end of a deer fence, or use the ladderstile, to follow a path leading down a ride in a spruce plantation. Climb another ladderstile onto open land, which the path crosses to reach Clashgour Bridge. This suspension bridge over the Abhainn Shira was restored in 1997.

4 On the far side of the bridge, rejoin the vehicle track, (which has forded both the Abhainn Shira and the Allt Suil na Curra), and continue to the right, up the rising ground to the outflow of Loch Dochard. The river on the right cascades down over a series of small falls, and the plantation to the left becomes a conserved area of old Scots pine and birch nearer to the loch. Go past a small corrugated-iron stable on the left. Then the well-maintained track crosses two burns on wooden bridges. Pause for a break on one of the promontories projecting into the loch and enjoy this wild, remote place. In early spring ravens perform complex aerobatics overhead.

5 On the return journey, retrace your outward route to the suspension bridge. Here you have a choice. If the water levels are not too high, ignore the suspension bridge, and ford the Allt Suil na Curra, either at the vehicle ford, or further upstream. Cross to the deer fence around the plantation opposite, and follow this uphill to a ladderstile. At the time of writing this stile was in an extremely poor state of repair though it was still possible to climb it on its right hand side. If it has not been repaired it is a short journey back to ford the burn again, and cross the suspension bridge to follow the outward route back to the Victoria Bridge car park.

Dipper

9

6 If you continue beyond the decrepit ladderstile a faint path follows the deer fence further uphill, until a broad ride appears on the left. Take the path, which goes down this ride. Very shortly it crosses a burn then joins a vehicle track through the plantation. This track is mossy, and gives very pleasant and comfortable walking. In early spring the woods resound with bird-song and pools beside the track are full of spawning frogs. In spite of the deer fence you may see red deer trotting away in front of you. Views of the surrounding mountains appear from time to time, particularly the 'Wall of Rannoch' ahead.

7 At the far end of this plantation is a wooden deer gate, with no ladder stile; if the gate is locked it unfortunately has to be climbed, which is not difficult apart from its height. After a short stretch of open ground, climb another deer gate and follow the track through another spruce plantation, winding uphill in a big curve to a wooden handgate at the far side. To the right are the ruined walls of a croft house. This is Druimliart, the birthplace of the Gaelic poet Duncan Ban Macintyre. A memorial in Gaelic beside the ruins commemorates him.

8 From here, the track winds downhill, with extensive views over Loch Tulla, and beyond to where the West Highland railway line leaves the road route to cross Rannoch Moor. Climb a ladder stile beside another deer gate and follow the track to the entrance to the Victoria Bridge car park.

Practicals

Type of walk: A pleasing walk, mainly on tracks, through a wild remote area.

Distance: 7 ½ miles / 12km (there and back the same way)
 8 ½ miles / 13.5km (the mainly circular walk)
Time: 4–5 hours
Maps: OS Explorer 377 / Landranger 50

NB: The walk to the loch is on a right of way. If you wish to leave the path during the stalking season, first telephone the stalker on 01866 82271

2

Rannoch Moor and Ba Bridge

Park near the access track to the picturesque Black Rock Cottage (the Ladies' Scottish Climbing Club hut), grid ref. 267532, where you can immediately join the West Highland Way (WHW). Or, if full, drive on a short way up the track to the White Corries ski centre car park, just below the long ski run and the chair lift, grid ref. 266526.

Ba Bridge

Today **Rannoch Moor** is a vast expanse of high moorland, interspersed with many boggy patches, pools, lochans, lochs and rivers. Once it was tree-clad and the bleached roots of pines are occasionally seen rising out of the peat. The huge open area has a background of fine mountains. Vegetation reaches knee height, kept so by the deer population and the weather, in contrast to the trees,

11

bushes and shrubs that thrive on the islands in the lochs out of reach of the browsers. In summer it is a place of colourful low-growing flowers, butterflies and dragonflies and, of course, midges and clegs. Be warned. In the depths of winter it is generally too inhospitable to enjoy a walk but on good days, all year round, it can be magical for those who enjoy high-level open spaces.

1 Join the West Highland Way and walk due south (right if you have to descend from the higher car park). At the Y-junction take the right fork, with the thistle sign of the WHW directing you along the track. Cross a small stone bridge and then leave the WHW to walk a narrow, very sketchy path, right, and go ahead to pick up a better path climbing steadily (left) up the moorland. This is the Old Military Road engineered by Major William Caulfeild. Work, by 25 officers and nearly 900 men, started on this stretch around 1752. Today it is narrow and it occasionally gets lost in the bog. Eventually it becomes overlaid by the WHW. In high summer the path passes through a fine flower garden and your boots crush the pungent bog myrtle in wetter areas as it traverses the lower shoulder of Meall a' Bhuiridh—the hill of the bellowing stags! Enjoy the magnificent views of Rannoch Moor stretching away in all its grandeur towards the mountains. Look for Schiehallion in the far distance.

Walk 2

2 At 1815ft / 550m you begin to descend towards the distant Wall of Rannoch, a high ridge of mountains, which stands beyond the many silvery pools of the moor. The way is occasionally lost but continue down until you can join the WHW. Turn right and walk on. Soon after a track leading off left, you pass another heading right into the moorland that gives access to the now ruinous Ba Cottage (Ba

meaning cattle). This must have been quite a haven when the routes over the moor were used as drove roads for taking cattle, on the hoof, to the markets in the south. Carry on to pass a plantation on the right and then continue to Ba Bridge over the River Ba. This is a delectable spot and one where you will want to linger and enjoy the dramatic gorge where birch and rowan clothe the sides of tempestuous River Ba. A little path off to the right, beyond the river, gives you a good view of the Ba Bridge. The view up-river to the Blackmount hills around the huge corrie is very fine.

3 And then begin your return along the WHW, ignoring the left and right turns, to arrive at the highest point at 1454ft / 443m. Look up left to see a rough unmarked cairn, a memorial to Peter Fleming, author and traveller. Beyond, the way continues downhill, is generally easy to walk, and returns you to where you have parked.

Goldenrod

Practicals

Type of walk: The Old Military road is a delight in spite of its boggy parts, with good views and interesting vegetation. Walking boots essential. The WHW is wide and reinforced, also with good views and lined with interesting flowers at the right time of the year. Save this walk for a fine day and after a dry spell.

Distance: 7 miles / 11.4km
Time: 3–4 hours
Maps: OS Explorer 384 / Landranger 41 and 50

NB The WHW is a right of way. Stalking takes place from Sept. 1 to the middle of Oct. If you require information tel. 01838 400225.

13

3

The Robbers' Waterfall, Glen Etive

Park in the lay-by, grid ref. 137469, near the end of the single-track road that passes through Glen Etive. This is accessed from the A82 by a well signed left turn before the A-road begins its descent of the Pass of Glencoe. The parking area lies approximately 10 miles / 16km along.

Glen Etive is a long narrow glen over which tower several fine Munros. The single-track road passes through scattered deciduous trees and then becomes more wooded and quite delightful as it continues to descend. The road accompanies the River Etive, its banks lined with trees and bushes, all the way as it hurries to pour its water into Loch Etive.

The Robber's waterfall is so named because it is thought that cattle thieves hid their stolen herds in the 'secret' ravine at the foot of the magnificent fall.

Waterfall on Allt Mheuran

1 From the parking place, turn right and continue for a few steps to take a gated track, on the left, signposted 'Hill Path'. Follow it as it descends through moorland dotted with deciduous trees. Here in early autumn devil's bit scabious, bog asphodel and golden rod give colour to the verges. Cross the high-level bridge over the River Etive, here very deep and stained with peat, as it surges between dramatic granite walls.

Walk 3

2 Bear right beyond the bridge and at the T-junction take the right fork to carry on. Pass in front of a white cottage, Coileitir, which has boarded up windows and padlocked doors. In front of the cottage stands a fine horse-chestnut tree. Walk on the way-marked path, which crosses several small streams on bridges of sleepers. Pass through a peaty area and then turn right to cross a wet area by stepping from stone to stone. This leads you close to the side of the Etive once more and the path improves as you continue on beside the river.

½ km

½ mile

3 The path then swings left away from the Etive to continue along the side of a tributary burn, Allt Mheuran, on a fine path with moorland all around. This brings you to two footbridges, one over the main burn and another over a parallel stream where the tributary has braided. Once across turn left and follow the path upstream. It is eroded in places and wet after rain but it is generally easy to walk and brings you to a charming small waterfall that descends, foaming white, into a deep turquoise-blue plunge pool. Mixed woodland on the opposite bank makes a fine backdrop. From here you can see the head of Loch Etive.

4 Carry on up a short distance to an area with virtually no turf, only finely ground granite and peat. From here two fairly distinct paths head on up the valley. The left branch carries on beside the river, climbing steadily until it is high above the hurrying burn. Part of

15

the way is a little 'white knuckle' as it traverses the edge of a steeply sloping grassy drop to the bottom of the ravine through which the Allt Mheuran races. It eventually brings you to the side of Allt nam Meirleach. The right branch is the path to Ben Starav. It is rough in parts but dry. This moves steadily away from the river. After about a ¼ mile / ½ km, you need to leave the path and walk ahead, remaining on the same contour, to arrive at the side of the Allt nam Meirleach, from where you have a good view of the Robber's waterfall.

5 If the latter tributary is not in spate you might wish to cross and walk on ahead to achieve a closer view of the fall on the Allt Mheuran. It plummets down a tree-clad ravine in a long graceful fall and at its foot plunges through Scots pine.

6 Then begin your return by re-crossing the Meirleach and walk on ahead to join the Ben Starav path to start your descent to the footbridge. Beyond, retrace your outward route.

Sneezewort and Devil's bit Scabious

Practicals

Type of walk: Easy walking until you reach the Allt Mheuran. Then the ascent to see the waterfall is harder, especially if you take the riverside path. But on a lovely sunny day it is a very satisfactory walk with fine views.

Distance: 4 miles / 6.5km
Time: 2–3 hours
Maps: OS Explorer 384 / Landranger 50

NB Stalking season from Sept. 1 to the middle of Oct. For information tel. 01855 851277. All dogs on leads.

4

Beinn a'Chrulaiste

Park in the huge car park at Kingshouse Hotel, grid ref. 259547. Access this from the A82 across Rannoch Moor. Just before it descends the Pass of Glen Coe, turn right down the short signposted road to Kingshouse.

Beinn a'Chrulaiste, at 2788ft / 857m a Corbett not a Munro, is nevertheless a fine hill to climb. It appears from the road through Glencoe as a great mound of a hill, but because of its situation has the most breath-taking views from its summit, and all the way down on the Glencoe side.

All the Kingshouses were built for the military, hence their names. **Kingshouse**, Glen Coe, was eventually used as a drovers' inn. Cattle for sale in the hungry industrial towns in the south, were driven, slowly, from the north of Scotland and the Islands. To keep the animals in good condition for sale, the drovers stopped overnight at 'stances' where the animals could be pastured and watered. These stances were about a dozen miles apart and Kingshouse was one. It was said that it was not a good inn but now is an excellent one. There was a stance at Inveroran (walk 1).

Buachaille Etive Mor from Beinn a'Chrulaiste

Walk 4

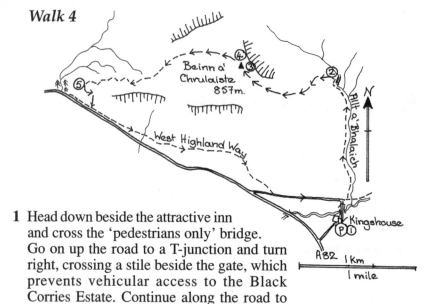

1 Head down beside the attractive inn and cross the 'pedestrians only' bridge. Go on up the road to a T-junction and turn right, crossing a stile beside the gate, which prevents vehicular access to the Black Corries Estate. Continue along the road to the bridge over the Allt a'Bhalaich. Do not cross but follow the clear path up the near side of the burn. The burn is delightful, with waterslides down granite slabs and little falls and deep clear pools; on a hot day you may not want to go any further. Carry on uphill, past a ruin on the far bank, until you reach a small gorge, where the river makes two right-angled bends.

2 Go up past the waterfall at the second bend and then leave the path and strike out across the moor, heading for the near ridge of Beinn a'Chrulaiste. The ground is covered with spikes of bog asphodel and heath spotted orchids with scattered cross-leaved heath and sundews, warning that in wetter weather it may be quite boggy. On gaining the ridge the walking becomes easier on woolly hair moss and slabs of rock; bear left at first to pick up traces of path, then wind round to ascend more steeply, zig-zagging where necessary. Here on a sunny summer's day you may be lucky enough to find mountain ringlet butterflies. Eventually the gradient eases and the vegetation becomes shorter and more tundra-like.

Mountain Azalea

18

Alpine Lady's Mantle

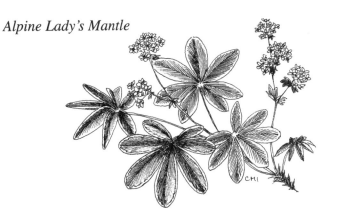

3 This is one of those hills with an ever-receding top. The cairn eventually does come into view, set on a small stony rise, and a few metres beyond is the trig point. Stop here for a while and admire the breath-taking view. To the south first the Blackmount and then the Wall of Rannoch hills stretch out into the wide watery expanses of Rannoch Moor, with Schiehallion beyond in the far distance. To its left lie the Ben Alder hills, then the Easains with Creag Meagaidh beyond, and in front the Blackwater Reservoir. To the north are the Grey Corries with the Mamores in front and Ben Nevis towering magnificently over all. Just below is Glencoe, with a fine view of Bidean nam Bian, and then across the valley dominating all the other hills is the spectacular seamed rocky bastion of Buachaille Etive Mor.

Mountain ringlet

4 From the summit, walk on northwards over stony tundra, heading towards Glencoe. Below you a wide ridge comes into view, with an area of pools and peat hags. Keep to the right to avoid these, and after a while pick up a path. This is intermittent at first but as you go lower it becomes more continuous and distinct. Avoid an area of craggy ground by keeping to the right of the ridge crest. Follow the path on down, heading for a small conifer wood, where the Devil's Staircase path leaves the main road.

5 Your path brings you down beside a fence to a gate; alas the gate is inaccessible as it stands on the far side of the fence. Turn left and walk along beside the fence, following it downhill towards the road. Then turn left and walk along parallel to the road for 110 yds / 100m to join the West Highland Way, where it comes over a stile from the roadside verge and climbs slightly, giving more fine views of the Buachaille. The Way then descends gradually towards Kingshouse. Cross a stile onto the minor road to Black Corries and turn left to reach the road junction by the gate. Turn right and walk down to the bridge and back to Kingshouse.

Large heath butterfly

Practicals

Type of walk: A strenuous climb because there is no continuous path, but there are no other difficulties. The return by the West Highland Way is easy.

Distance: 7 miles / 11.4m
Time: 4–5 hours
Maps: OS Explorer 384 / Landranger 41

NB Beinn a'Chrulaiste is on the Black Corries Estate where stalking takes place from September to the end of October (hind stalking till 15th February). Stalker's tel. no. 01855 851272. Please make contact if you wish to climb the hill at any of these times of the year.

Buachaille Etive Beag

Park in the recently constructed car park on the left of the A82 going north down Glencoe, just before the start of the Lairig Eilde path, grid ref. 188562.

Buachaille Etive Beag, the small shepherd of Etive, is somewhat dwarfed from Glencoe by its big brother Buachaille Etive Mor next to it, although it looks equally splendid in views up Glen Etive. However it would be a mistake to dismiss it on this account; it is less daunting and therefore more accessible for the walker and the views from its summit ridge down into Glen Etive and across to Bidean are unsurpassed. It lies entirely in National Trust for Scotland territory and therefore there are no access problems at any time of year.

Buachaille Etive Beag

Opposite the car park is a large beehive-shaped cairn. This is a **coffin cairn** on which a coffin was rested before the mourners journeyed on. The cairn was destroyed when the road was built in 1784, but restored by the National Trust for Scotland in 1992.

Walk 5

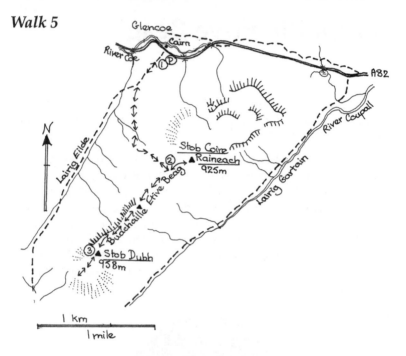

1 From the car park, walk up the path signed 'Lairig Eilde to Glen Etive'. The path is dry and stony and leads gently uphill at first. Then before it starts to descend to cross the burn, the Allt Lairig Eilde, look for a less well made path off to the left, which makes a rising traverse across the hillside. Follow it until you are past the crags, which are above and to your left. Curve round to cross a gully, with a burn, and ascend more directly uphill on the bank of another burn. The path is obvious here. It is scree in parts and eroded, but not difficult. Cross the gully and zig-zag up on the path to reach the lowest point of the ridge.

2 On gaining this high bealach, turn left up to Stob Coire Raineach. There are fine views from here back over Glencoe to the Aonach Eagach, and across the Lairig Gartain to Buachaille Etive Mor. Return to the bealach and continue climbing, south-west, along

Peregrine

the narrowing and steepening ridge. Cross a little top, and then enjoy the narrow high-level path, leading to a final short pull-up to the summit, Stob Dubh. The ridge continues beyond the summit and it is worth going on a short distance for the view down into Glen Etive. Look west across the Lairig Eilde to see the wonderful complex of peaks and crags of Bidean nam Bian, the highest mountain in the old county of Argyll. Here you might spot peregrines soaring overhead.

3 When you can tear yourself away, retrace your footsteps to the col and thence back down to the Lairig Eilde to your car. If you have been able to start this walk early in the day you will have a wonderful feeling of superiority brought on by meeting everyone else coming up as you are going down.

Practicals

Type of walk: A delightful climb for seasoned fell walkers.

Distance:	5 miles / 8 km
Time:	5 hours
Maps:	OS Explorer 384 / Landranger 41

6

The Lost Valley of Glen Coe

Park in the first car park, on the left, as you descend the pass of Glen Coe, just below the narrowing of the road, grid ref. 171569.

The Lost Valley (Coire Gabhail) is a wide, level, glaciated valley between two arms of Bidean nam Bian. Its entrance from Glen Coe is hidden where these arms come close together and the space between is full of huge boulders. The lost valley is a huge grassy and gravel area, the latter washed down by rivers. Here cattle could be kept safe from marauders, or stolen cattle could be hidden from their rightful owners. The MacDonalds used to hide cattle here.

The **Ring Ousel** is a summer resident and a bird of passage in spring and autumn. It lives among the heather and rocks of the moorland of our wilder hills, roughly above the 1,000ft (300m) contour. It is distinguished from the blackbird (where their ranges

The Lost Valley

overlap) by its white bib. In summer the male is sooty black. The female is browner and her narrower breast band is tinged with brown. When disturbed, or anxious about its brood, its angry *tac, tac, tac* is very harsh. It was this anxiety that revealed its presence on the way to the Lost Valley.

1 From the south-east corner of the car park, descend a path that soon becomes well pitched, to join the grassy, old road below. Turn left and follow this charming way to leave it at the next right turn. Stroll this mainly naturally reinforced way, steadily downhill, into a magnificent tree-lined ravine, through which flows the River Coe. Go on down a steep wooden ladder, and then a few rocks, to wind left round a large boulder. Curve right to cross the fine footbridge (constructed in 1960) across the hurrying burn.

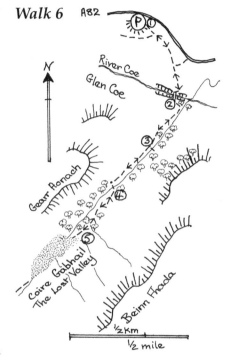

Walk 6

2 Climb up the continuing path soon to ascend a roughened, natural rock staircase out of the gorge to carry on through pleasing birch woodland, to come to a high stepped ladderstile. Beyond, the path heads up the edge of the Allt Coire Gabhail gorge. The way is well pitched, gravelled, or naturally stepped as it weaves round and over boulders, into the immense gorge. For a short distance it comes close to a steep drop down to the river and here children should be reminded to take care. Sometimes it is better to climb round, or over the great slabs, instead of remaining on the path along the edge.

3 Soon several fine waterfalls come into view, magnificent when the river is in spate. Carry on up. There are many little paths weaving between the boulder-strewn way and walkers should choose their own route through these. And then you arrive at the side of the

25

burn. Cross this on rough, natural stones or, you may wish to cross the larger boulders upstream beneath an enormous boulder. If the river is in spate the crossing should not be attempted and you should make this the point of return.

4 Go on up the far side of the river on the mainly pitched path. After a 100 yds / 90m or so, climb a slanting rock (a path does go round this boulder if you prefer). Then carry on up the stepped path through lush vegetation where golden rod, wood cranesbill, meadowsweet, water avens, wood rush and oak fern, colour the way. Here you might also spot a ring ousel. As you continue, ignore any little false paths that go off from time to time. Then climb, easily, through the wall of boulders that block the valley onto a green alp. Go across the alp and look down the far side to the Lost Valley.

5 You may wish to have your picnic here before you return by the outward route.

Wood Cranesbill

Practicals

Type of walk: A challenging walk through lovely dramatic scenery.

Distance: Nearly 3 miles / 4.5km
Time: 2–3 hours
Maps: OS Explorer 384 / Landranger 41 / Harvey Glen Coe

NB Glencoe is all National Trust for Scotland and therefore there is access all the time.

Loch Achtriochtan, Glencoe

Park in the lay-by on the south side of the A82 at the foot of the Pass of Glencoe, grid ref. 139567, beside the access track to the pretty cottage of Achnambeithach.

Some of the famous poets of the Glen Coe lived at **Achtriochtan** and suffered during the massacre.

Loch Atriochtan

Ossian was reputed to have been born beside the loch, a tranquil, peaceful pool, reflecting the fine buttresses of Aonach Dubh. Ossian's Cave can be seen above the tree-line of the magnificent buttresses but no one should attempt to reach it. Inside the cave the floor slopes steeply and it is doubtful if anyone could have lived in it. The unstable climb and the difficult descent was first completed by a shepherd in 1868.

Walk 7

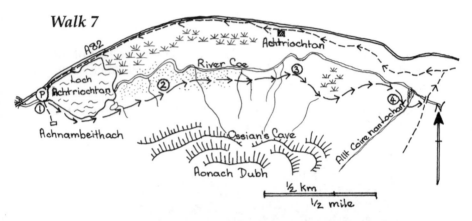

1 From the lay-by, cross the footbridge over the River Coe flowing from the foot of Loch Achtriochtan. Walk left over the flowery turf beside the river. Carry on along the side of the loch to pass through a gate and continue with a fence to your right. The pleasing shallow loch supports attractive water lobelia and in warm sunshine fish jump after flies. If the midges (mainly present during July through to September in dull, humid weather) allow, this is a place to linger. At the end of the loch are reedy flats where meadowsweet grows. Then, beyond, is the river flood-plain with pebbles and short cropped grass. Stroll on along an indistinct way. To avoid a large area of bog, move away from a branch of the river onto the lowest part of the steep slopes of Aonach Dubh. Look up the slopes to where each *Ravens* tier of rock is grassy and supports ash, rowan and birch. Carry on over a little hillock, which in high summer is bracken-clad.

2 Descend a little to come to the where the water of the side arm of the river ceases.

28

Continue over scree and below more bracken. Then you come close to the main river and here you need to wind right, on an indistinct path, walking slightly higher ground to avoid another boggy area. Walk on beside an old wall. The path then climbs above the flood plain over another small hillock. Remain well up and follow a little path through large patches of bracken, taking care not to trip on hidden stones. Each patch of bracken ceases where a stream bed, devoid of soil, cuts through.

3 Go through a gap in a derelict wall, where others have gone before, and walk on to pass through another derelict wall. Then you reach a large wettish area and, though this may be easy to cross after a dry spell, it is better to head right and edge round the marsh on slightly higher and drier ground. Stroll on to climb the next hillock and then descend left on a long ribbon of flat rock to ascend another hillock. From here go down, keeping keep right of the next hillock. Ahead are two more wettish areas and here you should wind right again, to curve round them on higher ground. Still curving you come close to the lovely ravine through which the River Coe hurries on towards the Loch Achtriochtan. Cross another wide rocky stream bed and walk on over hillocks, keeping parallel with the fenced ravine. Here a better path emerges and brings you to the edge of a steepish slope, down which you descend a bendy path.

4 Cross, as best you can, the very wide river bed of the Allt Coire na Lochan, which is only completely dry in a dry summer. Climb up the slope ahead to join the path from Coire nan Lochan to come to the sloping footbridge over the ravine. Cross and walk ahead on a good track to reach a cross of tracks. Turn left to start your easy return along the old road, here pleasingly reinforced, partly grassed and a joy to walk. At the time of writing you need to negotiate, with care, a damaged footbridge that has protective barriers at either end. Go through a kissing gate and look left to see where you have

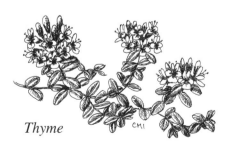

Thyme

29

walked earlier. High up is the gaping entrance to Ossian's Cave. At the Y-junction take the left fork. Cross a footbridge and then go on past a barn and the farmhouse of Achtriochtan. Join the farm's access track and continue on parallel with the road (A82). Head on a few steps to join the continuing footpath, part of a Millennium project, which enables you to walk on, safely. It continues beside the loch and well below the road. In summer the steep bank, on your right, is a wonderful floral garden. Look for common sandpipers, pied and grey wagtails about the shore of the loch. The path leads you to where you have parked.

Pied Wagtail

Practicals

Type of walk: First part is challenging. Best done in spring before the bracken becomes tiresome and after a dry spell.

Distance:	4 miles / 6.5km
Time:	3–4 hours
Maps:	OS Explorer 384 / Landranger 41 / Harvey Glen Coe

An Torr and Signal Rock

Park in the lay-by close to the deer gate into the woodland about An Torr, grid ref. 127566. This lies just beyond Clachaig Inn if driving from the foot of the Pass of Glen Coe along the minor road towards Glencoe village.

Signal Rock is believed to the place where a bonfire was lit at 5 a.m. on Saturday, 13th February 1692, to call the soldiers led by the Gaelic-speaking Campbells to slaughter the MacDonalds of Glencoe. All were to be put to the sword. For 12 days the Campbells were treated as honoured guests of the MacDonalds and when they did attack their hosts they violated one of the ultimate traditions of Scottish hospitality. MacIan, the clan chief, was killed as he rose from his bed to dispense more hospitality. His wife suffered many injuries and was left to die. Thirty-eight members of the clan were killed, including women and children, and many more starved to death or died of the cold as they escaped into the mountains or over Rannoch Moor.

Signal Rock

31

Speckled Wood butterflies are commoner in the south and west of Britain but they are spreading north. It is a butterfly of woodland rides and margins. There may be two generations, the first flying in May and June, the second in August and September. The green larva with white stripes feeds on various grasses.

Walk 8

1 Leave the roadside lay-by by the metal deer gate. Go past a National Trust for Scotland small pillar, signed An Torr. Pass through the next deer gate, one which you push and it self-closes after you. Carry on the lovely wide ride below mixed woodland, where speckled wood butterflies abound. At the Y-junction leave the track and take a path, going off right, signed An Torr. The way climbs a little and then winds right, ascending through delightful woodland. In a few minutes it brings you to the top of a huge flat crag from where you can look down into the forest and up Glen Coe and Gleann-leac-na-muidhe. After a short pause, enjoying the tranquillity of An Torr, return by the same route and go on along the continuing main track, by turning right.

2 At the T-junction, turn right to pass a sign directing you on for Signal Rock. Walk on through this peaceful woodland on a track

Speckled Wood

32

lined with needles from the conifer trees. At the next T-junction ignore the track going off left and follow a second sign for Signal Rock. The track soon winds round left and becomes bouldery. Ascend a little past some clear fell and go on to pass through a deer gate similar to the last one.

3 Climb up a hillock of conifers, still on the main track, then descend from it on a pitched path. Ascend again onto the next hillock by a reinforced stepped way. Wind right below Signal Rock. Carry on round and then ascend steps on the left to attain the top, in summer pretty with wild flowers. Today the crag is surrounded by the forest trees and there is no view and no one can see it from afar. It is difficult to imagine the part it played in the Massacre so many years ago. Then begin your return by the same route. Don't forget to turn left by the now second sign for Signal Rock in order to return to where you have parked.

Rowan

Practicals

Type of walk: Short. Easy in spite of its roller-coaster route. All within mixed woodland.

Distance: 1 ½ miles / 2.5km
Time: 1 hour
Maps: OS Explorer 384 / Landranger 41 / Harvey Glen
             Coe

9

Glencoe Lochan

Park on north side of the road, in a lay-by marked with a large blue P, at the north-eastern end of Glencoe village, grid ref. 104589. This is accessed from the lower end of the Pass of Glencoe by a narrow road, leaving right, just beyond Loch Achtriochtan. Or by turning sharp right off the A82 into Glencoe village just before you reach Loch Leven.

Donald Alexander Smith was a saddler's son born in Forres in 1820. He emigrated to Canada when he was 18 and rose to become governor of the Hudson Bay Company and High Commissioner for Canada. Later he became Lord Strathcona. He acquired the **Glencoe Estate** in the late nineteenth century.

The River Coe

Isabella, his wife, whose grandmother was a native American, was born and brought up near Hudson Bay. It is said that Donald wished to make her feel more at home, when they came back to Scotland, with the creation of the lochan and the planting of many trees and bushes that she was accustomed to in Canada. Sadly Isabella was not happy in Glencoe in spite of the beautiful surroundings. It is also said that she didn't enjoy the Glencoe weather! Eventually she and her husband returned to Canada for good.

The estate woods were bought by the Forestry Commission in 1950 and subsequent plantings have retained the woodland appeal.

1 Walk back over the bridge across the River Coe and, just beyond, turn left into fine deciduous woodland. Ignore the right turn and carry on the track as the way continues parallel with the river. A few steps before the next junction, by a small water hydrant post, turn left onto a narrow path through the trees. Wind right and then descend steps to the water's edge. Look upstream for a dramatic view of the spectacular gorge through which the river surges and 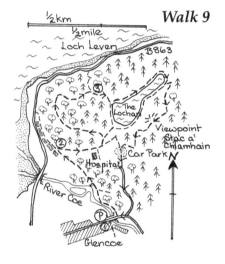 rages. Return to the main track and walk on. Pass behind some bungalows, which face towards a sparkling Loch Leven and the hill of Beinn a' Bheithir.

2 Opposite a house named Hillcrest, take a sharp right turn to walk a track that climbs steadily and brings you to the side of Glencoe House, once Invercoe House, and now Glencoe Hospital. Just beyond, turn left at the T-junction and wind round right. Go through a gate into Forest Enterprise woodland and on to a wide track. Almost immediately turn left to climb up through mixed woodland, following a green way-marker banded with yellow. The way is lined with Gaultheria, a flowering bush that grows wild in Canada. Go on climbing under Western Hemlock and Cypress, and on to a seat to pause and take in this most beautiful woodland. Then

descend quite steeply. Climb up
again to a viewpoint where, to
your left, is a picnic table and a
fine view of Loch Leven, its
islands and Ballachulish. Then
carry on round the hillside
through deciduous woodland to
a T-junction.

Heron

3 At the small man-made lochan,
turn left to enjoy a wonderful view of the Pap of Glencoe. Wind
left round the lochan and, when on the far side, look for a left turn
that climbs and then winds rapidly, right, following a green post
with a blue band. This is quite a steep climb and the seat two-
thirds of the way up is most welcome. Continue on to a Y-junction.
Sit on another seat here, to enjoy the view of Loch Leven where it
narrows. Go down a steepish path and at its foot wind left and
walk on to descend steps into a car park. Bear left across the parking
area and walk downhill to join a road coming from the hospital.
Turn left and go on down to walk between fine gateposts and out
onto the public road. Turn right and walk past the track taken at
the outset of your walk, then cross the bridge over the River Coe
to return to your car.

4 Before you leave Glencoe village you might like to walk up the
road, opposite to where you have parked, signposted 'Massacre
Memorial'. A short way along, on the right, pass through ornate
gates and climb the path to stand by the railed monument, erected
in memory of MacIan, chief of the MacDonalds of Glencoe, who
died in the massacre of Glencoe. It was erected here by a direct
descendent of MacIan in 1883.

Practicals

*Type of walk: Delightful. Lots of climbs and descents, but
always through magnificent woodland. Good tracks. Fine
views.*

Distance: 2 ½–3 miles / 4–5km
Time: 1–2 hours
Maps: OS Explorer 384 / Landranger 41 / Harvey Glen Coe

Ballachulish Slate Quarry and Am Meall

Park in the large car park beside the VisitScotland Centre, grid ref. 085586. To access this, leave the A82 at the loop road through Ballachulish.

The Ballachulish slate quarry was opened in 1693, just one year after the Glencoe Massacre. It reached its heyday in the nineteenth century, and was finally closed in 1955. The arch was built in 1822, and is just over eighty feet high. It was used as an incline to transport slate from the quarry to the shore-front. Originally there were two of these arches, but the other was demolished to make way for the A82 road.

The Arch, Ballachulish

1 Leave the car park, cross the loop road, and enter the slate quarry through the wooden gates. A very short 'all abilities' path leads around part of the quarry, well supplied with information boards. The lochan created by the flooding of the lower excavations has a pleasant shore, where seats and picnic tables are provided in a very

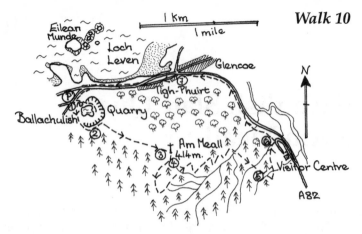

sheltered spot. Return to the entrance, but just before the gates take a path of slate chippings, which leads steeply up to the left and skirts the quarry. It passes through gorse, heather, small rowans and birches. Soon there are wonderful views out over Loch Leven and Loch Linnhe to the mountains of Ardgour. Then the path levels out on a grassy alp, where another path branches off to the right. Ignore this and follow the route up, which bends round to the left and continues uphill, just set back from the quarry.

2 Continue through a fallen gate which lies on the path, the latter now fenced from the quarry on the left and with a plantation on the right. The ground is more open here, with scattered birch trees and in early spring, a carpet of bluebells. At an old stone dyke (wall) the path leaves the quarry edge and strikes off up the hill to the right, following the wall between the plantation and the open hillside. The walking is steep but pleasant, with grassy steps. A few boggy areas, in spring, are full of mayflowers (ladies' smock), whilst underneath willow bushes there are mats of primroses. The views open up all the time. Behind, the long view over the loch, with the slate quarry and Eilean Munde (the burial isle) immediately below; to the west, Beinn a' Bheithir (the hill of the thunderbolt); and ahead, the Mamores and the Pap of Glencoe start to emerge over the skyline.

3 The telecommunications tower sited at the top of Am Meall comes into view. Shortly before reaching it, cross a deer fence by a ladder stile, with a warning notice of underground electrical cables. The panoramic view from the top of the hill (1343 ft / 414m) is rather

38

marred by this installation, but by dropping down a few metres towards the Glencoe side, the magnificent vistas up the glen to Bidean nam Bian and across to the Pap of Glencoe and Sgorr nam Fiannaidh can be enjoyed uninterrupted. A ladderstile over the deer fence beside the tower leads onto a vehicle track into the forest.

4 Initially the track follows the ridge between Glen Coe and the glen south of Ballachulish, but eventually it starts to zig-zag down into Glen Coe, with the occasional view of Aonach Dubh and Loch Atriochtan. In places the dark spruce plantation gives way to lighter, bright green larch, and at one point a bridge leads over a most beautiful burn, where the water has carved potholes which are filled with flat blue-green pebbles of slate. The track continues to zig-zag steeply down into the glen.

5 There is a small 'short cut' footpath off to the left, going down beside a burn, then crossing it, which cuts off the final bend in the track. Turn left onto the track again and walk on until it emerges from the forest, through a gate which prevents vehicle access, into a clearing just behind the National Trust for Scotland Visitor Centre (which you might like to visit) and Camp Site. Then turn left onto a forest track, which bends round to the right and is shortly crossed by a way-marked footpath. Turn left onto this.

6 This link path, opened in 2002, between the camp site and Glencoe Village, avoids the nearby A82. It provides a very pleasant walk through the woods, with timber bridges over two burns, the second of which is the pot-holed burn crossed higher in the forest. The

Primroses

remains of a dwelling called Inverrigan, on the left, have a National Trust plaque and, inside, a small wooden cross which is a private individual memorial to 'the Clansmen', the MacDonalds of Glencoe. Soon the path runs right beside the A82, which you cross to continue along the pavement for ½ mile to the road junction at Glencoe Village.

7 Then re-cross the A-road to walk on along the old road, past the cottages of Tigh-phuirt. Eventually you have to cross and rejoin the pavement of the main road for another ½ mile to reach the road sign for the Ballachulish loop road, with the huge slate arch on the left. Cross the main road again and join the 'all abilities' path leading from the arch towards Ballachulish. Go over the loop road to return to the car park.

Goldcrest

Practicals

Type of walk: Delightful way around the quarry. Steepish climb to An Meall and a well contoured zig-zag path down to the A82. Some road walking but all on pavement.

Distance:	5 ½ miles / 9km
Time:	3 hours
Maps:	OS Explorer 384 / Landranger 41

Cuil Bay, Appin

Park before the metalled road turns sharply to the right, grid ref. 978553, where there are several places to park just above the shore. To access this take the A828 from Ballachulish towards Oban, past where it leaves the coast at Kentallen and reaches the rather scattered settlement of Duror. At the village school, a minor road leads to the right to the settlement of Cuil.

Duror Ardsheal was home of James Stewart of the Glen, famously hanged for the **Appin murder** which he did not commit. His main crime was to be brother of the clan chief, living in exile in France, and to have supported the losing side in the Forty-five Rebellion. Since it was a Campbell who was murdered (Colin Campbell of Glenure) on Ardsheal land, James was held to represent his clan and accordingly was tried before a court of Campbells at Inveraray, found guilty and hanged. There is a memorial to him near Ballachulish Bridge.

Back Settlement Bothy, Ardsheal

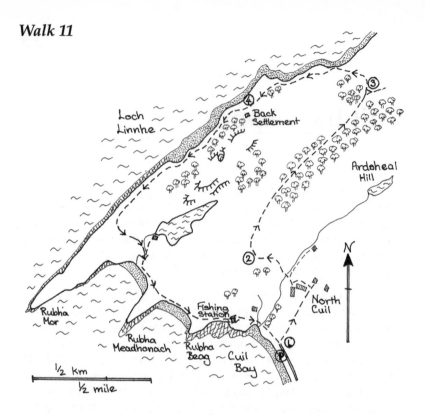

1 Leave the shore, following the metalled road round to the right. When this turns into a rough track, turn left, passing a steading with a Dutch barn, and go through a gate with a letter-box beside it. Follow the track as it winds uphill to the left, until it levels off. Here a track forks off to the left; the main track leads up to a white house ahead. Follow the left fork; unfortunately its very good surface degenerates quite quickly, and it becomes an ancient grassy track leading off across the hillside through some old turf field boundaries. At times the track is rather more like a watercourse, but it is possible to find drier ground at either side. In early summer the hillside is covered with heath spotted orchids.

2 Step across a metal gate in a broken-down fence. Beyond this the path continues across the hill through bushes of bog myrtle, with fine views across to Ardgour. Pass through a gap in an almost ruined stone wall, and continue across moorland, with a small lochan down to the left and beautiful views up Loch Linnhe ahead. The path soon enters a wood of hazel, oak, birch and the occasional wild cherry, on the north-west slopes of Ardsheal Hill. Butterwort grows in profusion. The wood soon becomes mainly hazel, showing the unmistakable signs of ancient coppicing. In spring it is a mass of primroses. A small metal gate leads into another wood, this time with larch on the left and the coppiced hazel on the right. Progress on the next short section of path is difficult, because of some fallen branches, but soon more open ground is reached, covered with bog myrtle and orchids. There are fine views ahead up Loch Linnhe to the narrows at Corran.

Heath Spotted Orchid

3 The small path meets with a much larger track. Follow this to the left, through a metal gate down towards the shore. To the right is a lovely bay, where the policies of Ardsheal House come down to the sea. Continue down a very grassy track which bends round to the west, then loses itself in the lush grass and clumps of yellow flags. Climb over a low stone dyke and walk along the pebbles of a small beach, then step easily over a wire fence at the far side. Not far from the shore you soon strike a clear path. It leads around, just above the shore, to an expanse of grassy pasture, merging into the pebbles at the top of the beach. A small restored cottage, marked on the map as 'Back Settlement', nestles against the higher ground, with the ruins of other buildings beside it, and views straight across Loch Linnhe to Glen Tarbert on Ardgour.

4 Follow the shore around, just at the top of the beach. Oystercatchers and common sandpipers are frequent here. The shore provides the driest walking, but eventually the best route should be picked over the small shoulder of land towards the lochan seen earlier in the

Goosanders

walk. There is another small bothy beside this, from where a path leads down to the shore again. Walk round the grassy land at the head of several bays on an increasingly visible footpath, until you reach a track, leading past a small fishing station with nets spread outside. This track goes all the way to the metalled road at the head of Cuil Bay; the only obstacle is a locked gate, easily climbed, or the fence at the side, which can almost be stepped over.

Practicals

Type of walk: Can be a rather wet walk after rain. Wonderful views.

Distance: 4 miles / 6.5km
Time: 2 hours
Maps: OS Explorer 376 / Landranger 49

12

Kinlochleven Waterfalls and Loch Eilde Mor

Park in Kinloch-more, grid ref. 188622. This lies across the river from Kinlochlev-en. Follow signs for Grey Mare's Fall and Visitors' Car Park. This is north-west of the main road, beside a simple white church. To access this, turn right in Glencoe along the B863 to Kinloch-leven.

Kinlochleven is a strange town built for workers at the British Alumin-ium Works and looking incongru-ous in its beautiful setting. Huge pipe-

*Grey Mare's Tail,
Kinlochmore*

lines come down the valley behind the town, bringing water from the Blackwater Reservoir. The works are now closed and the enormous building houses a micro-brewery and also the Ice Factor, probably the best and most innovative climbing wall in the country.

The Grey Mare's Fall or **Grey Mare's Tail Waterfall**, was once known as the Falls of Kinlochmore. They are considered to be one of the best of the great waterfalls of Scotland. When the Aluminium Works was built it was believed that the falls would lose much of their water and that the scenery round about would be spoilt, deterring tourists from visiting. Neither happened. No water was taken from the falls and, between the Kinlochmore Works and the fall, is an idyllic tree-clad hill.

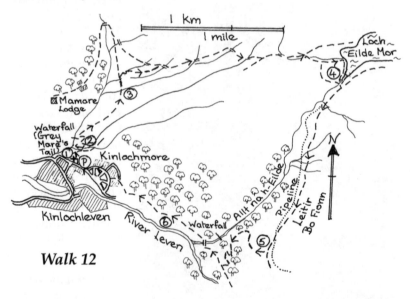

Walk 12

1 Leave the car park by the path running north away from the road into deciduous woodland. Turn left along a well-made path surfaced with chippings and fit for wheelchairs. Climb the gentle zigzags to a viewpoint where the falls can be seen through the trees. This is as far as a wheelchair can go. Carry on down steps beyond the viewpoint into a delightful woodland valley. In spring it is carpeted with bluebells, violets, wood sorrel and wood anemones. Cross a bridge over the burn, turn left to walk the short distance down to the meeting of this burn with the larger Allt Coire na Ba

46

just beyond the foot of the splendid waterfall. The fall is in a cleft and you cannot easily see all of it but it is nevertheless spectacular.

2 Retrace your steps to the bridge but do not cross. Continue up the valley beside the burn until you reach a waymarked junction, where you should turn left. Climb steeply, with care, up out of the wood on a zig-zagging path, which is a little eroded in places. Enjoy the fine views back down to Loch Leven as you ascend higher. Above the trees there is a T-junction where you should turn right and cross

Woodsorrel and Feather Moss

the grassy hillside towards Coire na Ba. The mountain at the head of the corrie is Stob Coire a'Chairn, with Am Bodach to the left of it and Na Gruagaichean to the right; they form a dramatic ring of peaks, part of the fine Mamores Ridge.

3 Cross two sparkling burns, the first on stepping stones, the second on stones and then turn right at another junction. This clear well-made path takes you up across the hillside, through a deer fence, to join the landrover track, which goes conveniently along the south side of the Mamores. Turn right and follow the track as it contours the hillside, to come over a slight rise and down towards Loch Eilde Mor. Before you reach the loch look on the right of the track

Common sandpiper

for a stalkers' path marked by a small cairn. Follow this path down to cross a burn and where it divides take the less obvious left branch along the bank of the burn to the loch. There are pebbly beaches and a headland with some good rocks to sit on. Maybe the only sound in this remote place will be the calls of sandpipers.

47

4 Continue south above the loch shore to a small dam over the outflow, which you should cross. Go up to join another path, which runs along the hillside to the south of the loch, and turn right. This wide path contours high above the valley of the Allt na-h-Eilde, with a pipeline running along a few metres further down the hillside. The pipe was put in to take water from Loch Eilde Mor to the Blackwater Reservoir in the next valley and ultimately to generate electricity for the aluminium works. There are good views down Loch Leven again, and across to the Aonach Eagach's jagged ridge ahead.

5 After 1 ¼ miles / 2 km look for a clear stalkers' path descending the hillside on the right. Go down the path, which is beautifully constructed in long zig-zags so that the gradient is nowhere difficult. The path enters birch and oak woodland lower down. Go through a gap in an old wall and slightly uphill to join a path coming in from the left. Cross an open area, where there is a good view, to the right, of another splendid waterfall then, shortly after re-entering the trees, cross a substantial wooden bridge over the Allt na-h-Eilde and turn left along the far bank. The Allt na-h-Eilde joins the River Leven here in a welter of falls and foaming pools, and there is yet another waterfall on the valley side opposite.

6 Continue through the open deciduous woodland, a joy in spring when it resounds with bird song. Take the next path on the right to contour above Kinlochleven, then go through a deer fence and above an electricity substation. At a T-junction with a reinforced path turn left and go on down to a road. Cross and walk ahead down another road through houses. Turn right at the end, round a grassy lawn planted with fine trees, then right again at the T-junction at the end. Follow this road, where there is pavement, all the way back to the car park.

Practicals

Type of walk: Delightful. Mainly on good paths. There is a steepish climb up from the Grey Mare's Tail.

Distance: 5–6 miles / 8–9.5km
Time: 3–4 hours
Maps: OS Explorer 392 / Landranger 41

NB You are requested to stay on paths during the stalking season Aug. to mid Oct. For information tel. 01397 732362.

13

Loch Ossian

As there are no public roads to Loch Ossian you will need to reach the start of the walk by taking the West Highland Railway to Corrour station. The line runs from Glasgow to Fort William and you should check the timetable to make sure that the train stops at Corrour, grid ref. 356664.

The West Highland Railway Line was opened in 1894 and is considered one of the most scenic routes in Scotland. Corrour station stands on a high, extensive moorland plateau 1344 ft / 410m above sea level, surrounded by dramatic mountains. Some of them are Munros (mountains over 3000 ft / 915m) that entice many to climb them.

In 1891 Sir John Stirling Maxwell bought **Corrour** and started to create 'a gentleman's paradise'. Until 1910 guests arrived at Corrour Station and then were conveyed by pony trap to a boathouse on the shore of Loch Ossian. Here they boarded a steam yacht and it chugged up the beautiful stretch of water to Corrour Lodge. Once the estate road was constructed from the station along the north

Loch Ossian

side of the loch, cars could be brought by train and these were then used to carry the guests.

At the time of writing the **Corrour station** buildings, which had provided bunkhouse accommodation and the Station House restaurant, were closed indefinitely. There are no toilets at the station but there is a little wooden waiting room and a glorious view.

The boathouse is now a **Scottish Youth Hostel** that runs an eco-friendly regime. Its site on the edge of the loch is magnificent and it is a welcoming sight after a day on the mountains. It lies a mile from the station along a well reinforced track.

Corrour Lodge burnt down, accidentally, in 1942. In 1999 it was rebuilt, as **Corrour New Lodge**, in an interesting modern style, its owner and staff providing the facilities needed for many outdoor activities, making use of the surrounding moorland, mountains and loch.

1 At Corrour Station, cross the railway line and leave the station buildings to join the estate road, walking east. The way continues over moorland where, in high summer, an array of wild flowers colour the harsh environment. On either side of the track, which was once forested, look for the skeletal roots of ancient trees that have risen from the peat. Soon the lovely Loch Ossian, with its islands and magnificent backdrop of mountains, including Beinn Eibhinn to the left and Ben Alder to the right, come into view.

2 Pause at the T-junction of tracks and look ahead to see the youth hostel, tucked snugly under a group of trees. Then turn left to walk on, with a good view down the loch. Go through

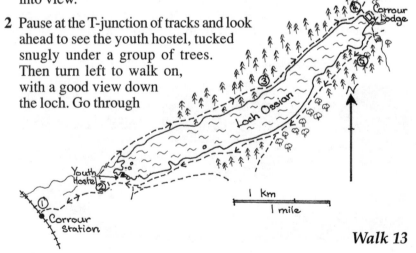

Walk 13

50

a deer gate beyond which rowan, birch and Scots pine have been planted, and willow now thrives well, all safe from hungry deer. The track takes you over a tiny ravine where a myriad of flowers grow, including the beautiful St John's wort. Follow the track as it moves into a plantation of Norway spruce, with faint glimpses of the loch through the trees. Through the foliage slip goldcrests, robins and red polls. Soon the track comes to the side of the loch and the views are spectacular. Here you might wish to pause for your first break, or walk out on a tiny promontory with a row of Scots pine along it, an idyllic corner.

3 Continue on, close to the water, where in high summer the banks are lined with purple, pink and white foxgloves. Look for grey wagtails, siskins, spotted flycatchers and great spotted woodpeckers as you continue. Look also for gold-ringed and common hawker dragonflies hurrying from side to side of the track.

4 At a junction of tracks, turn sharp right to pass a memorial to Sir John Stanley Maxwell (1866–1956) whose research work at Corrour provided the information which led to the afforestation of much of upland Britain. Carry on winding round the foot of the loch. Pass a boathouse, with turf on its roof. Go on with tiny glimpses of New Corrour Lodge. Cross a substantial burn and where the track divides, take the right branch. Pass two pretty white cottages and then go on in front of several newly built dwellings.

5 Continue on the pleasing track through mixed woodland and

Foxglove

51

lined with a variety of rhododendrons, which flower splendidly in spring. And then the delightful, easy-to-walk track, descends to the side of the loch. Go through a gate and carry on with the water lapping beside you. The loch side of the track is lined with alder and an occasional quivering aspen. Deciduous trees, mainly birch, clothe the steep slopes to your left. Down on the shore of the loch are tiny little sandy beaches. Carry on to a cross of tracks. The right one leads to the youth hostel, which you might wish to visit, or carry on to come to a T-junction of tracks, where you bear left on to the track to the station.

Black-throated diver

Practicals

Type of walk. An idyllic walk on a lovely day. The loch and the station are high above sea level and this could make for a cold walk unless suitably clad. Level walking on dry tracks.

Distance: 9 miles / 14.5km
Time: The hours between your trains
Maps: OS Explorer 385 / Landranger 41 and 42

Inchree Waterfalls and 'Caulfeild's Road'

Park in the car park, grid ref. 030635. This lies at the road end in the small village of Inchree. This small hamlet lies off the A82 between Onich and Corran Ferry.

Inchree or Glen Righ Falls are a dramatic staircase of eight falls on the Abhainn Righ, a little river that hurtles down through densely wooded banks. Glen Righ means the king's glen.

Inchree Waterfalls

1 With your back to the information board, walk ahead from the car park. Bear left for a step and then right as directed for the 'waterfall walk'. Continue on to cross a footbridge and climb through mixed woodland. Where the way opens out there are seats and from these you have good views down to Loch Linnhe. Ascend the reinforced path and follow it as it turns a corner from where you have your first view of the spectacular falls on the Abhainn Righ. As you go on up, particularly if the leaves have fallen, look down right to see more superb

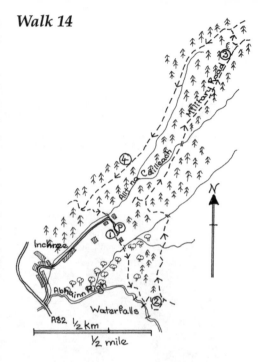

falls on the turbulent burn. Then stand on the special viewing platform for yet another grand view of the raging falls.

2 Continue on up the pleasing path to join a forest road, where you turn left and begin to descend. At a cross-road of tracks, turn right and ascend a narrow way, strewn with needles, that follows the route of another old military road, engineered by Major William Caulfeild. It climbs steadily through conifers, its banks lined with moss, wood sorrel and hard fern. Cross the footbridge or ford the Allt nan Cailleach and climb quite

Kestrel

54

steeply as the path winds up through the forest over quartz and through heather. The way then levels and goes past a seat, with the forest opening out before you. From here you can look up to the open hills.

3 Descend a little to come to a quarry, where you wind left and follow a sign for the 'forest walk'. Carry on down and then curve left, following the green posts with red bands. Walk on gently down below clearfell. Ahead is a fine view along Loch Linnhe to Appin. To your left is a very deep, narrow, steep-sided ravine, lined with glorious vegetation. Here you might spot a kestrel hovering, watching for a movement among the plants.

4 Then the track descends into more conifers. On a bend look for the picnic table and seat set on a hillock on your right. From the hillock you can look down a ride to see the Inchree waterfalls once again. Opposite the hillock a sign directs you left, downhill on a steepish, narrow path, through conifers. At the next seat you can still glimpse the waterfalls, but when the trees grow the view will be lost. Go on down the slope. Cross a footbridge and bear right at the sign for the car park.

Hard fern

Practicals

Type of walk: A delightful walk, almost all way on good tracks. Good for an early morning walk or one in the evening.

Distance: 3 miles / 4.75km
Time: 2 hours
Maps: OS Explorer 384 / Landranger 41

15

Cow Hill, overlooking Fort William

Park in the free car park at Fort William, grid ref. 097736. If coming from the south, it is the first signed car park, on the left, beside Loch Linnhe.

Cow Hill as the name implies was once the common grazing ground for cattle of the town's inhabitants. Today the Scottish forestry commission together with the local community manage the woodland of alder, birch and willow. Through these lovely trees roam roe deer, pine marten and the all too infrequent red squirrel. The peat trail that traverses the southern flank of Cow Hill was traditionally used by local crofters who dug and collected peats. These were stacked and left to dry, to provide fuel for the winter. Today red grouse feed on the heather moorland and meadow pipits abound on the hill. From the viewpoint there is a wonderful panorama of the hills, glens and sea lochs around Fort William, including the highest hill in Britain, Ben Nevis.

On Cow Hill

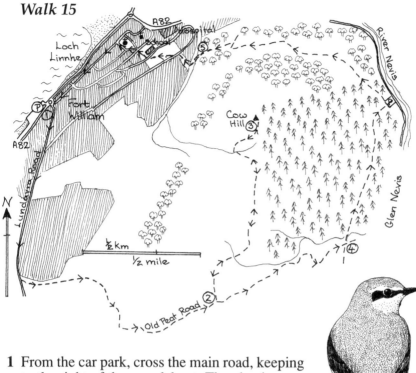

Walk 15

1 From the car park, cross the main road, keeping to the right of the roundabout. Then begin your ascent of Lundavra Road opposite as it winds right. Continue climbing steadily until you reach the end of the houses (¾ mile / 1.2km). Cross the cattle grid and take, on the left, the signposted peat track. This is an excellent hard surfaced, well contoured track which winds uphill before bearing right. Follow it as it then winds left to continue climbing through the heather moorland.

Wheatear

2 At the Y-junction, turn left for Cow Hill as directed by the delightful way-marker. The track, still reinforced, leads you to a gate and a stile with a dog gate. Follow the roller-coaster way until you reach the telecommunication pylon on the hill. Continue on a few steps for a fine view down over Fort William, strung out around a huge curve in the loch, Loch Eil, running west from the head of Loch Linnhe.

3 Return along the track to climb the stile and then go on to the Y-junction, where you turn left. After continuing over the open moor

57

for a little way the track enters, by a kissing gate, the Nevis forest. From here there is a wonderful view of the Mamore hills, especially fine when dusted with snow. The continuing path is a joy to walk, though steep in places. The narrow way is littered with pine needles as it descends through birch, young larch and spruce. Lush grass, heather and bog myrtle edge the path on either side. As you drop down the views are excellent. Then go down a flight of steps to a signpost at the bottom. Here, turn left (for the town centre) to walk a wide, very pleasant forest track.

4 The gently descending track brings you to a small gate beside a much larger one and then goes on to a signpost. Just beyond is a small car park. Here take the left turn along a well surfaced way. Climb steadily uphill through the lower wooded slopes of Cow Hill. Carry on climbing, now with open views of the town to the right and wooded slopes to the left, which climb to the top of the hill. After passing a seat on a hillock, begin your descent through trees, following the path as it winds right. Then in a few steps take the next left turn and carry on through open pasture to descend to a footbridge.

5 Cross the footbridge over the burn and walk on to join a road and continue ahead. Where the road begins to turn left, go down a ginnel on the right of the road. This leads to a long flight of steps, which drop steeply, right, to a road. Cross and continue down a slope and then descend more steps. At the bottom, turn left to walk past a children's play area, on your left. At the road walk on past a school and turn right down another stepped track to the next road. Bear left and just before a church, on your right, turn right to join Fort William's main street, pedestrianised and full of interesting shops. Turn left and walk on until you come to the large roundabout. Cross with care to return to the car park, beside the loch.

Practicals

Type of walk: A good walk on reinforced tracks. Fine views from several high points.

Distance: 5 miles / 8km
Time: 2 ½ hours
Maps: OS Explorer 392 / Landranger 41

16

Glen Nevis
and the Lower Falls

Park at the Glen Nevis visitor centre, grid ref. 123729, where there are toilets. This is reached by an easterly turn off, a 'no through road', signposted Glen Nevis, off a small roundabout on the A82 at the north end of Fort William.

The Lower Falls of Nevis descend for 12m below the road bridge that crosses the Water of Nevis. The burn is split in two by a huge boulder and then the two streams rejoin, one fall overlapping the other before thundering on through the Achriabhach gorge. From here you cannot see Ben Nevis but the quartzite top of Sgurr a' Mhaim, one of the Mamores, is visi-

The Lower Falls, Glen Nevis

59

ble. Sometimes the falls are named Polldubh falls or Achriabhach falls. The names of the two dwellings, once farms, passed on this walk.

1 From the parking area, climb up the bank to a footpath along the side of the River Nevis, a lovely river with a good population of trout and salmon. Turn left and walk downstream to take the suspension footbridge over the river. Turn right and start your long walk upstream through the glorious glen, with the lower slopes of Ben Nevis towering overhead. Look out for dippers as you go and also look for the path up the hill, which was the supply route to the weather station on the summit and is now the usual route of ascent. Do not turn left here, but keep on the riverbank. Ignore the footbridge to the youth hostel and also the track, left, and continue on beside the river, which is lined with alders, where great spotted woodpeckers linger.

Walk 16

2 Ignore the stile ahead and wind right to walk round the outside of the fence above the river. Then descend to cross a burn (the first of many) on convenient stones. The pleasing path, still outside the fence, leads you to a stile, which you do take to cross the fence and continue on a soggy way over the corner of a pasture to cross a stream. Then stroll on a delightful grassy trod along a river terrace. Carry on until you pass a magnificent beech, with seven or eight trunks. Just beyond is a large walled area with huge beeches and sycamores, well spaced around the wall. This is the old graveyard of the Camerons of Glen Nevis, Ach-nan-Con, field of dogs. Most of the graves are unmarked. Take your first break in this peaceful corner. From here you have a great view of Five Finger Gully and a long white waterfall descending in one stream above the slopes of Carn Dearg.

3 Walk down beside the far wall of the cemetery, in the direction of the river, to go through a gate and turn left along the path beyond. When you reach a burn with a deep pool, where the path should be, make a short diversion right and then left to rejoin the path on the far side. Walk on beside the river with the fence to your left. Cross a muddy section of the riverbank on convenient stones.

4 Go through a gate gap in the wall ahead and carry on along a grassy trod beside a wide stretch of the now shallow River Nevis where you might spot a goosander flying downstream. Then follow the path as it moves a little away from the river and into alder woodland and then on through birch woodland. Soon the path moves down towards the river again and through more alders. Pass through the next stile and continue away from the river on the rising path to pass between two buildings, Polldubh, to join a wide well made track. Stride on, now high above the river. Go through a gate to pass a sheepfold, to your left, and then through the next gate and descend to the narrow road.

5 As you cross the road bridge, look left to see the dramatic Lower Falls on the Water of Nevis just before the river passes under the bridge. Then look over the other side of the bridge to see where the river hurries angrily along, deep down in its gorge. Once over the bridge, wind right. Stroll on along the road for a short distance and, when opposite the first dwelling, Achriabhach, take a wide track into the forest and climb steadily through conifers. As you go, enjoy the wonderful view of the glen below and the flank of Ben Nevis.

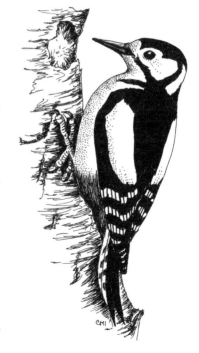

Great spotted woodpecker

Ignore the track coming in on your left and walk on the high-level way. Pass through more conifers and then follow the track as it begins to descend and continues through clearfell, which enables you to see the path traversing the fell opposite, on its way to the summit of Ben Nevis. Ignore the first track going off right and further on notice the West Highland Way coming in on your left.

6 Head on and at the next junction of tracks and a signpost, turn right in the direction of the visitor centre. Walk the narrower track through conifers and follow it as it winds, descending easily to carry on to a kissing gate. Walk straight ahead. Pause along this track to look up the glen for a superb view of the hills. Join the road and stride the pavement, left. About 100m along, cross the road to go through a wall gap. Follow the path beside the river to arrive at the visitor centre.

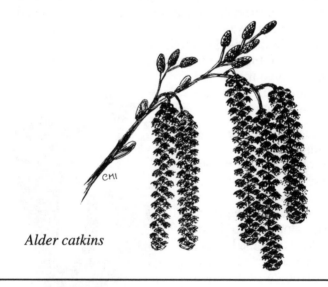

Alder catkins

Practicals

Type of walk: A walk beside a lovely river, through a glorious glen, with dramatic views throughout. A walk not to be missed.

Distance:	8 miles / 13km
Time:	4–5 hours
Maps:	OS Explorer 392 / Landranger 41

17

Stob Ban
and Mullach nan Coirean

Park in the Lower Falls car park, grid ref. 145683, on the right beyond Achriabhach, just before the road takes an acute angled bend and crosses the river. To reach this take the minor road up Glen Nevis from the roundabout at the north side of Fort William.

Stob Ban and Mullach nan Coirean are two of the ten Munros linked together to form the high ridge of the Mamores, which encloses the south side of Glen Nevis. These are spectacular peaks, well supplied with good stalkers' paths that make access relatively easy. Fit walkers can do the whole ridge in a day, but there is much to be said for splitting it up and thus enjoying several wonderful walks.

Stob Ban

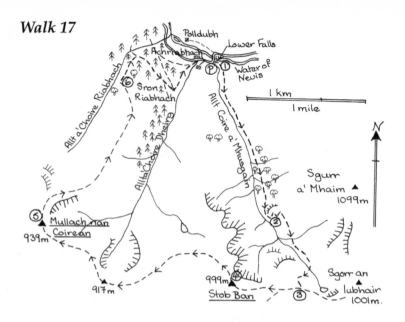

Walk 17

1 Leave the car park by the entrance and turn right along the road. Go down to the bridge and admire the Lower Falls. Then return towards the car park but, just beyond the bridge, go over a stile on the left, with a sign 'Mamore Grazings. Dogs on leads'. Follow the well-worn path turning right across the field. In summer look for dragonflies, especially golden-ringed dragonfly, which patrol the field edges. The path soon begins to climb and proliferates; it can be quite wet in places so pick your way carefully. All the paths join up again as you come over the lip of Coire a'Mhusgain, where the gradient eases. The view ahead is spectacular, almost alpine in character. Stob Ban at the head of the valley is rocky and angular and seems dauntingly high; the valley itself is narrow and grassy with steep sides and scattered mature birch trees. Continue along the pleasant narrow path to go round a steep craggy shoulder with the burn now well below to the right.

2 Immediately beyond this crag, take the path which zig-zags up the steep hillside, not the obvious (but misleading) small path which goes straight on but is blocked by stones. After the zig-zags the path contours high on the side of the upper corrie, eventually crossing a burn and then leading up. Look left from here for a glimpse of the delightful Lochan Coire nam Miseach, cradled below the crags of Sgorr an Iubhair. If you want to visit it turn left just below the ridge and contour round to the lochan. Spend time enjoying this high, secluded spot before retracing your steps up to the ridge.

3 From here Stob Ban looks less daunting. Turn right along the ridge towards it and keep to the high ground on a walkers' path, ignoring the stalkers' path which goes off down the hillside to the left. Climb quite steeply with some easy scrambling to the rocky quartzite summit and enjoy the superb view of mountains in all directions.

4 Leave the summit of Stob Ban by a ridge going north and descend over quartzite boulders at first, then easier ground to a col. Notice where the rock changes from the white quartzite which gives Stob Ban its name to the red granite of Mullach nan Coirean. Also notice the remains of a wall which you can see crossing the entire ridge; most likely an estate boundary. Follow the path along the scrambly crest of the next top (easier than by-passing it) then over a gentle grassy top and onto the rounded stony summit of Mullach nan Coirean. It looks a long way from Stob Ban.

5 Walk north across the stony summit on a clear path, keeping the headwall of Coire Dearg to your right. The path curves round to the north-east to descend a long spur between Coire Dearg and Coire Riabhach. At first it is stony and steep but then eases and becomes peaty. At a deer fence corner carry straight on with the fence to your right. The slope becomes steep again and the path

Golden ringed dragonfly

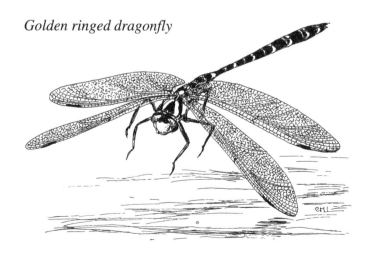

quite eroded and it is better to take to the heather and make your own way down.

6 Climb a stile over the deer fence into birch woodland and continue downwards on the clear but now very wet path. The Allt a' Choire Riabhaich hurries down a steep slope to the left. The path soon enters conifers and fortunately becomes drier. Descend steps onto a forest road and turn right. At a Y-junction take the left branch, then at a hairpin bend take a way-marked path on the right which winds down beside a burn to rejoin the track at the edge of the forest. Walk out to the road at Achriabhach and turn right to return to your car.

Mossy Cyphel

Practicals

Type of walk: A challenging walk for seasoned fell walkers. Good stalkers' path up to the ridge, then walkers' paths. Very wet and boggy for a short distance in the top of the wood on the way down from Mullach nan Coirean. No stalking so access is fine all year.

Distance:	7 miles / 11.4km
Time:	6–7 hours
Maps:	OS Explorer 392 / Landranger 41

18

Glen Nevis Gorge and An Steall Ban

Park at the very end of the road in a good car park, grid ref. 167691. To reach this, drive along the minor road up the south side of Glen Nevis from the roundabout at the northern edge of Fort William.

The Nevis Gorge was famously described by W. H. Murray as "the finest example of its kind in Great Britain. The immense walls to right and left are wooded in pine, oak, birch and rowan. These

An Steall Ban

sprout in profusion from the crags, giving the rock gorge a Himalayan character not seen elsewhere in this country. The apparent height is greatly increased by the wide flash of Steall waterfall, which shows through the V-shaped cleft on top".

The Nevis Gorge was identified as a suitable site for a **hydro-electric scheme** but fortunately this was successfully opposed so that the many hundreds of visitors each year can still enjoy its unique beauty.

An Steall Ban, the waterfall beyond the gorge, is 350ft / 106m high, the third highest in Scotland. It has the most spectacular situation. It appears at first glimpse to be on the Water of Nevis but is actually on a tributary, the Allt Coire a' Mhail. The first view of it as you emerge from the gorge is breathtaking.

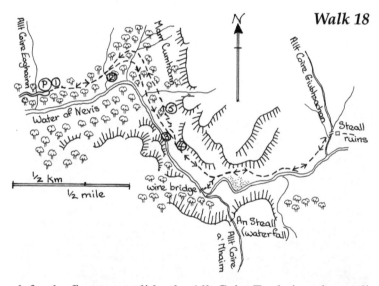

1 Look for the fine water-slide, the Allt Coire Eoghainn, descending the slopes of Ben Nevis above the west end of the car park. Then walk out of the east end of the car park, following the sign to Corrour and Rannoch. Note, but do not be too alarmed, by the various notices warning you of the dangers of the gorge, path and surrounding hillsides. You should, however, be wearing proper footwear. The path is very popular and you are likely, in summer, to be among many other people going the same way. In winter the path can be covered in ice and then it can be very difficult. Quite near the start, ascend a natural rock staircase and then cross a wide shelf, which has been blasted out of the cliff.

2 Beyond this, follow a yellow way-mark, which directs you left away from a small path going down into the gorge. Look on the left for an obscure path coming down, more like a watercourse at this point; this is your return path but do not be put off, most of it is very easy to walk. The trees are mainly oak and birch, with some Scots pine. These, together with the constant sound of waterfalls below, adds to the considerable atmosphere of the gorge. Look for the spectacular potholes and the gouged and waterworn walls of the ravine when you can see them between the trees.

3 Suddenly the tree-lined gorge ends and you emerge into the peaceful hidden meadows of Steall. Ahead of you is the most magnificent waterfall, a curtain of white lace, which seems to be at least half the height of the mountain, An Gearanach, behind it. Walk along the path, which edges the meadow, then curves right and brings you to the 3-strand wire bridge over the Water of Nevis. Cross if you want to try out your gymnastic skills, but you will have to come back again because this walk stays on the near side. Continue up the valley to the ruins of Steall beside a delightful tumbling burn, the Allt Coire Guibhsachan. The path continues up into wilder, bleaker country to Corrour Station and beyond, but this walk returns from here.

Siskin

4 Walk back along the meadow to the entrance to the gorge but just before you reach it look for an indistinct path on the right. Follow this through a gap in the remains of a wall after which it becomes more obvious. Climb its tight zig-zags up a grassy slope between the sheer wall of the gorge to your left and a steep crag to the right. Finally the path reaches a flat grassy shoulder, marked by a cairn, which is below the cliff and well above the gorge.

5 The views from here are splendid. Continue round the edge of the plateau, curving to the right. Do not be misled by a boggy rake

Coal tit

going down left as you approach the trees at the far side of the plateau; your path goes up slightly and then along into the edge of the trees. It is a good path, an old drovers' path, and though now rough in places is perfectly clear to follow. It crosses two watercourses and then descends gradually, becoming very rough for the last few metres before it reaches the main path, which you rejoin just east of the rock shelf mentioned previously. Turn right and retrace your steps to the car park.

Practicals

Type of walk: The path has been upgraded and is very good at the start but does become rougher and quite scrambly in places further into the gorge. There are some considerable drops so care must be taken especially with children.

Distance: 3 ½ miles / 5.5km
Time: 2 hours
Maps: OS Explorer 392 / Landranger 41

19

Ben Nevis

Park in the Visitor Centre car park, grid ref. 123729, or in the small car park at the end of the road at Achintee, grid ref. 126729. To access the car park at the visitor centre, take the road up Glen Nevis from the roundabout at the north end of Fort William, and drive up the glen. Alternatively continue north on the A82 across the bridge over the River Nevis and take the next turn on the right. Follow this road to its end at Achintee.

Ben Nevis, 4400 ft / 1343m high, is not only the highest mountain in Britain but also one of the most spectacular. Unfortunately the side it presents to Fort William and up which the 'Tourist Track' climbs seems only big and bulky: its magnificent cliffs are hidden round the other side. The Ben is formed of andesite, a rough grey rock formed by the cooling of acidic lavas, whilst the surrounding hills are formed of reddish granites. The view from the top on a

Ben Nevis and 5-finger gully from Glen Nevis Walk

clear day is unbelievable, so much higher than all the surrounding mountains that it seems as if all Scotland is spread out below you. Clear days, however, are not the norm; the summit is in cloud for around an average of 300 days a year, gales are frequent and the mean annual summit temperature is below freezing. The weather station on the summit of Ben Nevis was built in 1883 and operated for 20 years; the path now called the Tourist Track was built as a pony track for access to it. Gardyloo Gully was so called because it was where the people manning the Observatory discarded their waste.

Walk 19

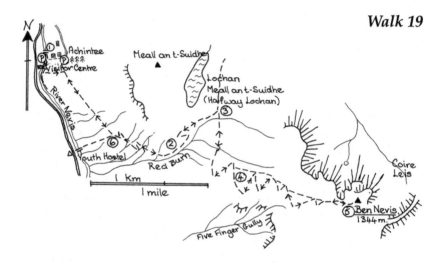

1 Walk north from the visitor centre car park to cross the river by a footbridge. Turn right and follow the clear path back along the riverbank, signed 'to Ben Nevis'. Take the path, also signed, which goes left at the next junction and walk up the field beside the wall. At the top, join the path, which comes along from the car park at Achintee and turn right. This path is well-made and well-maintained, paved and stepped for much of its length. There are bridges over the larger burns. It makes a long ascending traverse across the side of Meall an t-Suidhe, the hill which hides Ben Nevis from Fort William, then climbs steeply with hairpin bends in places into the valley of the Red Burn.

2 Carry on up the zig-zags (don't be tempted to cross the burn and go up the other side, this just makes the erosion worse) and over a

72

lip onto the gentler ground of the col, which holds Lochan Meall an t-Suidhe, often called Halfway Lochan.

3 At a large cairn turn right, keeping on the main tourist track. It is broad and clear but very rough and rocky. It zig-zags up the hill at a fairly constant gradient. Ford the Red Burn in a rocky gully, which is a popular place for a refreshment stop.

4 After the next hairpin the path splits but either branch works; the left branch is steeper and more eroded and the right branch is easier and more pleasant but zig-zags more. Cross near the top of the deep Gardyloo Gully. Take care especially if there is snow on the ground when cornices may have formed. The summit plateau, when finally reached, is amazingly flat, with splendid cliffs to the left. It is somewhat disfigured by the ruins of the observatory, a shelter, a memorial cairn and a cairn plus trig point; consequently it would be hard to miss even in mist. It is also usually quite busy. Look out for snow buntings here, they are remarkably tame and will even come for crumbs. Enjoy the amazing view.

5 Return the way you came, taking care in poor visibility; it's quite easy to become disoriented on the summit and a wrong direction can lead to disaster. The path is edged with large stones but in snow these may not show and in mist they may not stand out. Footprints in the snow could be going anywhere. If caught by bad weather the compass bearing to follow is 231 degrees for 150m from the trig point at the summit, then 281 degrees until off the plateau and onto the descent. The two gullies to beware of are

Snow buntings

Gardyloo Gully on the right and Five Finger Gully on the left; both are close to the path and hold cornices in snow. In summer and good weather, however, finding the way is very straightforward. Go down the path to the cairn and junction above Lochan Meall an t'Suidhe. Continue down the main path, the left branch, over the lip and down the zig-zags above the Red Burn.

6 At a junction the left branch goes straight downhill to Glen Nevis youth hostel, grid ref. 127717, while the right branch continues fairly gently down to Achintee, where there is a back-packers' hostel and a pub. Just before reaching this there is the left turn back down to the visitor centre.

Practicals

Type of walk: All on clear paths. It is not a difficult climb, but it is very long. It is a full day's expedition. As you descend you will meet ill-equipped people all the way, still going up and asking if they are near the top yet. Most of them make it or sensibly turn back before it gets dark. Just because there is an obvious well-made track all the way up doesn't mean that this is a mountain to treat lightly, even in good weather. Of course in bad weather or winter conditions it can become a very difficult and dangerous proposition; and it is worth remembering that the temperature 4,400 ft / 1343m above sea level is much lower and the wind much stronger than it is in the glen. Be ready to turn back should conditions deteriorate.

Distance: 9 miles / 14km, 1343m of ascent.
Time: 7 hours (1 ½ hours is the fastest time in the Ben Nevis fell race)
Maps: OS Explorer 392 / Landranger 41

20

Coire Leis and
the north face of Ben Nevis

Park in the car park at the end of the track, grid ref. 144764. To access this, drive north from Fort William along the A82. Two km past the Mallaig turn, take a very minor road on the right, signed Torlundy. Cross a bridge with traffic lights over the railway and turn right immediately along a track signed North Face car park.

   The north side of Ben Nevis has some of the most spectacular cliffs on the British mainland, riven into corries and gullies with snow in their recesses for much of the

North Face
of Ben Nevis

year, and separated by dramatic pinnacles and ridges. This side is hidden from the Tourist route up from Glen Nevis, and anyone approaching from that side has no idea of all this grandeur until the summit is reached. Then the view down over its abrupt edge is stunning, but for the best views this walk is recommended. It could be combined with Walk 19 as an alternative route up The Ben; just carry on along the path past Lochan Meall an t-Suidhe until it joins the main path at a cairn, and then turn left up the long stony track to the summit.

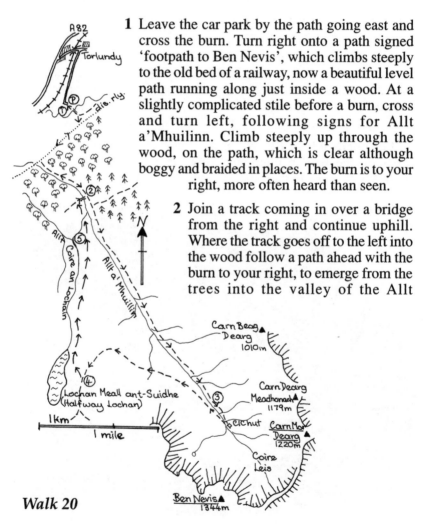

1 Leave the car park by the path going east and cross the burn. Turn right onto a path signed 'footpath to Ben Nevis', which climbs steeply to the old bed of a railway, now a beautiful level path running along just inside a wood. At a slightly complicated stile before a burn, cross and turn left, following signs for Allt a'Mhuilinn. Climb steeply up through the wood, on the path, which is clear although boggy and braided in places. The burn is to your right, more often heard than seen.

2 Join a track coming in over a bridge from the right and continue uphill. Where the track goes off to the left into the wood follow a path ahead with the burn to your right, to emerge from the trees into the valley of the Allt

Walk 20

76

a'Mhuilinn. The path is rough and can be wet in places but is very obvious. Follow it for about 1 ¾ miles / 3km up the valley, enjoying the magnificent views of the north side of Ben Nevis. This is the side that few tourists ever see, all superb cliffs, buttresses and corries; it gives a much truer picture of the nature of the mountain than the well-used track on the other side can ever do. The top of the valley (Coire Leis) is closed by the fine arete joining Carn Mor Dearg to The Ben.

3 The path climbs up to the left of a rocky step, and the valley narrows ¼ mile / ½ km before you reach the mountain rescue post and the Charles Inglis Clarke Climbing Club Hut at grid ref. 167723. Cross the river wherever you can and join the path on the other side; there is no point in going right up to the hut unless you want to shelter by it whilst you eat lunch! Turn right on this new path and head out of the valley again. Look out for ring ousels along this stretch in spring and summer, although you are more likely to hear their three-note call or their blackbird-like alarm 'chacking'. The path is small but quite distinct, and contours below the spectacular cliffs, gaining a little height just before it turns the corner out of the valley. The views down towards Fort William and beyond are fine. Follow the path round to a wide boggy col; Lochan Meall an t-Suidhe, often called Halfway Lochan, is below to the right.

4 The path descends slightly and at the lowest point turn off it to the right, heading for the north end of the lochan. Then make your way down the gently sloping hillside beyond the lochan into the valley of the Allt a'Mhuilinn,

Harebell

77

with the Allt Coire an Lochan on your left. There are bits of path but nothing definite and the ground can be quite boggy after rain, but it is not difficult. Head for the top of the forest where the Allt a'Mhuillin enters the trees, where you may see deer.

5 Come to a stile over a deer fence and cross it; there is no path on the other side and it is something of a flounder, but in about 220 yds / 200m you will reach a forest track. Turn right, cross the bridge over the Allt a'Mhuilinn and immediately turn left on the path by which you ascended. Follow this back to the car park.

Buzzard

Practicals

Type of walk: Most of this walk is on clear paths, but on the return to the valley of the Allt a'Mhuillin from the lochan there is no proper path and so some direction-finding ability is needed. It is quite rough underfoot in places, and does climb from just above sea-level to 1950 ft / 600m and this must be borne in mind. Strong walking boots and waterproofs, map and compass and so on must all be taken.

Distance: 7 miles / 11.4km
Time: 5 hours
Maps: OS Explorer 392 / Landranger 41

21

The Caledonian Canal: Corpach to Torcastle

Park in the public car park, grid ref. 096768, on the left of the Station Road at Corpach. To reach this leave Fort William on the A 82 going north. About a mile out of the town turn left at a set of traffic lights, onto the A830, the Road to the Isles, signed to Mallaig. Corpach is about two miles along this road. Cross the River Lochy and then the Caledonian Canal and turn left for the station and the Snowgoose Bunkhouse.

The Caledonian Canal links a series of lochs running along the fault line of the Great Glen. It was completed in 1822, as part of a project to open up the Highlands in the aftermath of the Jacobite Rebellions. The engineer was Thomas Telford. It provided shelter for the Navy from French privateers, then became a success for commercial craft from 1880 on. Now it is only used by fishing

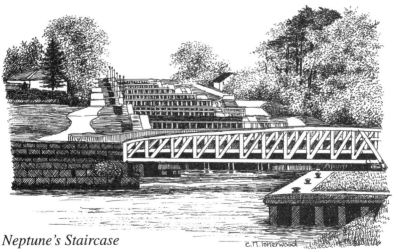

Neptune's Staircase

boats and leisure craft, providing an easier and quicker journey from west to east coasts. It is 60 miles / 97km long, with 22 miles / 35km canalised, the rest being open lochs. It has 22 locks, including the splendid flight at Banavie, which is called Neptune's Staircase. The highest point is Loch Oich at 106 feet / 33m above sea level.

1 Continue down Station Road and cross the railway at a vehicle crossing with flashing lights to warn if a train is approaching. Turn right and walk down to the end of the canal, where there is a quay with a lock-keeper's office and a lighthouse turret. Cross the canal on the last set of lock gates, which open into the sea in Loch Linnhe. If these are open and cannot be crossed use another set further up the canal. Turn left and walk along the towpath, which is also the Great Glen Cycle Way, in the general direction of Inverness. The path is lined on the right with fine mature beech trees, between which are glimpses across the loch to Fort William and the huge bulk of Ben Nevis, with the pipelines for the Aluminium Works coming down its side above the town.

2 After 1 mile / 1.5 km, at Banavie, first the railway and then the road cross the canal on swing bridges. Go through a kissing gate and cross the railway carefully, looking both ways for trains (there are no flashing lights here) and exit through another kissing gate. Emerge onto the A830 and cross with even more care as it is much busier than the railway. Continue on the towpath to walk uphill beside Neptune's Staircase, which is a splendid flight of eight locks in succession. Then the canal is poised above the wide River Lochy, Lochaber's best salmon river. Enjoy the views across to the mountains between the

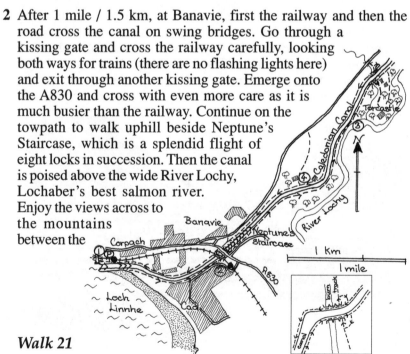

Walk 21

80

mature trees on your right. In spring there are primroses and wood sorrel on the banks of the canal, and many mallards with ducklings on the water.

3 About 1 ¾ miles / 3km further on the River Lochy veers away to the right. Look for Torcastle Cottages below to the right. Look carefully to see a burn and then a track passing under the canal. Immediately after crossing them take a very small path down the embankment on your right, and turn right onto the track. Go under the canal, through the right-hand arch of the aqueduct (the other two are occupied by the burn), and come out below a weir on the burn. Turn right again and follow another small path up the embankment, cross a wooden stile and gain a gentle path (see inset map). Turn right and walk back towards Banavie and Corpach. Go through a kissing gate beside a metal field gate and then through several other gates. There are birch woods lining this bank, and a small lochan feeding into the canal. The mountain views are more open. Look for sandpipers in summer.

4 Eventually the path joins a broader track, which leads to the moorings above Neptune's Staircase. Cross the A830 and the railway again and follow the path onward by the canal past a marshy area full of kingcups and yellow irises, back to Corpach.

Marsh marigolds and Water avens

Practicals

Type of walk: A very easy level walk for a quiet day.

Distance: 6 miles / 9.5km
Time: 3 hours
Maps: OS Explorer 392 / Landranger 41

22

Linear walk through the Lairig Leacach

Parking: There is space for about five cars in a small area on the left where the track crosses the old railway, the Puggy Line, grid ref. 255788. Do not park in any of the passing places as you drive up the track. If the parking place is full, or if forestry operations make the use of it impossible, you will have to return to the tarmacked road below Corriechoille and turn right towards Insh. About 110 yds / 100m along here at grid ref. 253806, there is a parking place for the scout camp, where space is normally available. To reach these two parking areas, drive along the minor road on the south side of the River Spean. Going north from Fort William, turn right into the road, signed to Corriechoille and Killichonate, just before the Spean Bridge Hotel. Continue until you reach the end of the tarred surface just before Corriechoille Lodge. At present it is still possible to drive up the reinforced track past the lodge and on for a further a mile to just before the forest gate.

Cruach Innse
and Sgurr Innse Lairig Leacach

The track through the **Lairig Leacach**, an ancient drove road through the mountains, is a right of way. The path goes on to Corrour, where it links up with other paths from Glen Nevis and Kinlochleven and runs on south to Rannoch and beyond. It gives access to the very remote northern fringes of Rannoch Moor. At the bothy you feel a long way away from motorised transport. The pass is surrounded by high mountains, the Grey Corries enclosing it to the west, and the two Innses to the east.

1 Set off from where you have parked and carry on up the track through a kissing gate beside the deer gate into the forest. Walk on up the track with a deep ravine to your left, lined with birch, hazel and larch, and full of small birds. The track winds round to the right, and now the forest has been opened up there are extensive views over the Spean valley. Beyond the clearfell, the trees are mainly mature larch, with a burn to the right of the track. At the top of the forest, exit through a deer gate, shortly followed by an ordinary gate, onto open fell.

2 To the right are the steep lower slopes of the Grey Corries, not grey but green with birch wherever there is enough soil to root among the rocky buttresses. To the left, grass slopes down to the Allt Leachdach, which descends in a series of sparkling waterfalls. Cross a stout wooden bridge over the Allt Leachdach. Continue up the glen as it opens out ahead, with the splendid rocky spur, Creag an Fhireon, protruding into the glen, providing a fine backdrop to the falls and pools of the burn,

Corriechoille

Allt Leachdach

Cruach
▲ Innse
857m

Stob Coire
Gaibhre▲
958m.

Sgurr
Innse
809m ▲

Stob Coire
nan
1121m. ▲ Ceannair
1123m.

Stob Coire
Claurigh▲
1177m.

Bothy

1 Km

1 mile

Walk 22   972m.▲
Stob Ban

83

and a long series of waterfalls descending from Coire na Ceannain, on the right. Watch for peregrines circling above. At the right time of the year you might hear the whining cry of young ones waiting for food.

Peregrine

3 Cross a ford on stepping stones, widely spaced but firm, and then go on to the top of the pass, with slabs of rock and boulders on both sides. The dramatic shape of Sgurr Innse dominates the view ahead, with Stob Coire Easain peeping over its shoulder. Cruach Innse, more rounded than its sibling, towers on the left. Descend gently with the view improving, to a tiny lochan on the left. Then the bothy comes into view, with the fine conical peak of Stob Ban, of the Grey Corries, behind it, and a burn beyond. Here, beside the bothy, might be the place to eat your lunch before you retrace your steps, enjoying the views in the opposite direction.

Practicals

Type of walk: An easy one on a generally good surface. It is used by cyclists. The way rises gradually to a high point of 500m. It is a right of way and can be walked at any time of year. The mountain views are excellent.

Distance: 8 ½ miles / 13.5km
Time: 5 hours
Maps: OS Explorer 392 / Landranger 34 and 41

23

Monessie Gorge
and Cille Choireil

There is a space which will take 3 or 4 cars just before the bridge over the River Cour, grid ref. 247811. If this is full drive on for another ¼ mile / ½km and park in the parking space for the Scout Camp before the bridge over the Allt Leachdach, where there is usually room, grid ref. 253806. Do not use passing places along the narrow road for parking. To access the parking area turn right off the A82 from Fort William as you come into Spean Bridge, onto the minor road along the south side of the River Spean, signed to Corriechoille and Killiechonate. Drive along this road for about 1 ¾ miles / 3km.

Bridge on the Puggy Line

85

Monessie Gorge. This spectacular gorge has two waterfalls, one above the suspension bridge and one well below it. This walk visits both, but the best views are to be had from the West Highland Railway line, which clings to the extreme edge of the gorge for all its length.

In 1925 the '**Puggy Line**', a narrow gauge railway, was built for the transport of materials during the construction of the dam at Loch Treig and for servicing the massive tunnel excavations to take water from the loch to Fort William. It closed in 1977. Today the remnants, especially the bridges, are dangerous and should not be traversed but the trackbed makes a good path.

Cille Choireil (Church of St Cyril) was first built in the sixth century by Cyril, nephew of St Columba. It was replaced in the fifteenth century and restored in the 1930s. From it there are superb views across to the Braes of Lochaber.

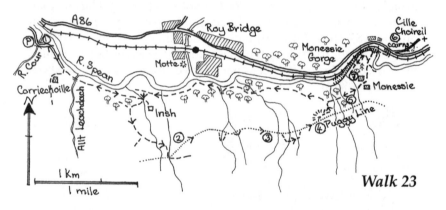

Walk 23

1 From the parking area cross the bridge over the River Cour and walk on along the road, continuing on ahead where it becomes a track at the turn to Corrie-Choille farm. Carry on past the Scout Camp, on the left, and cross the Allt Leachdach on a substantial bridge. Go through the deer gate (with a notice saying Private Road, Obey Country Code, Shut all Gates) and on past Insh Cottage on the right. The River Spean, wide and shallow here, keeps company with you on the left. Look for dippers, grey and pied wagtails, and flocks of siskins in the birch trees. Then the Spean bends away to the left and the track forks; take the first branch on the right, just before the main track crosses a burn. Curl round to the right,

winding uphill beneath mature trees. Keep to the main track, which carries on upwards, ignoring a less-used track to the right. At the next junction take the left branch, cross the burn on a high culverted embankment and curve round to the right into an area of old gravel excavations. Where the track turns left at the end of these look for the line of the old railway, the Puggy Line, just below the track, and go down onto it for some delightful walking.

2 Look down towards Roy Bridge below, on the other side of the Spean, where you can see the huge mound of the motte and bailey beside the River Roy. Contour round the hillside to reach a ravine which the old line crossed on a girder bridge. The remains of this are extremely flimsy and cannot be crossed. Instead take a small path along the edge of the ravine, on the right, and follow it up past a telegraph pole until it goes gently down to the water's edge. Cross on flat pebbles and bear left up the opposite bank. Follow the small path back to rejoin the Puggy Line and continue. At the next ravine, where progress along the girder bridge is barred by a wooden fence, take a small path to the right, which slants gently down to the burn. Cross on convenient stones and climb the easy path sloping back up the far side to rejoin the line.

3 Continue round the hillside, above the ruined cottage of Chlianaig, walking a clear path through bracken that grows over the hillside and on the old line. Don't trip over piles of old sleepers left since the rails were taken up. The next burn but one, the Cruaidh Allt, is another ravine with waterfalls, and this time there is no obvious path. Here climb up to the right well before the fence across the

Grey wagtails

87

line, using animal paths through the bracken. At the top edge of the bracken the gradient eases; here turn left and go along to the edge of the ravine, which is now shallow. Cross the burn on flat slabs of rock where there is a convenient birch tree to hold on to. Follow clear animal tracks at the far side and contour the hill until you have crossed two more small burns, then descend steeply down a pleasant grassy rib to rejoin the old railway line and carry on.

4 Leave the line when you reach a small hut and pick your way carefully down the hillside to the flat top of an old spoil heap, made bright in summer with cushions of thyme and tormentil. At the east end of the spoil heap join a track which curves steeply down to a deer gate. Go through, turn right and immediately go through another.

5 Follow the continuing track through birch woodland and out into sheep pasture and then down to the farm of Monessie. Go through the gate, turn left through another gate by the garden, then curve right downhill to another gate. Walk through the pasture beyond and through another gate to the riverbank, where you turn left. Where the main track turns right, go straight ahead down a sloping path into an oak wood and along to a fine suspension bridge over the River Spean. This is the top of the Monessie Gorge; there is a waterfall to your right and you can see the West Highland railway hugging the cliff on the far side. Cross the bridge and turn right through a small gate to walk a track beside the railway, lined with meadowsweet, vetch, harebells and bedstraw in summer. Cross the railway on the bridge and turn right to wind round between buildings and up to the main road. The cottage on the left is the place to ask for the key to the church of Cille Choireil, which is well worth a visit. Cross the road with care and walk up the minor road opposite to the church, which is perched on a shoulder of the hill above the wide valley of the Spean. Enjoy the peace and quiet of this place.

6 Retrace your steps to the suspension bridge and cross, walk up through the wood, and near the top of the river terrace take a small path going sharply back on your right. Follow this through the bracken into oak and pine woodland, then turn left round the corner of a fence. The path becomes a delightful wide mossy track; go on along it above the gorge until you can look back to see a fine view of the Monessie Falls through the trees. There is no point in going further as the path comes to an end by a concrete installation on the bank of the river.

7 Retrace your steps to the main track and return through the farm to the deer gate where you joined it. Continue along the lower track over open pastures. You can see the Puggy Line high above on the hillside. On your right mature trees line the steep slopes above the river. Descend into fine oak woodland, past the well-kept cottage of Inshwood, go through a deer gate and uphill to cross a burn on a wide bridge. The track then goes back down to the bank of the Spean, which is wide and peaceful here where, in summer, sand martins and swallows chase flies above it. Go through another deer gate into, first, pasture and then, arable land. The white farm of Insh appears on the hillside to your left. Below it, turn left into a well-used track, go through a deer gate, turn right to cross a bridge and rejoin your outward track. Return to your car.

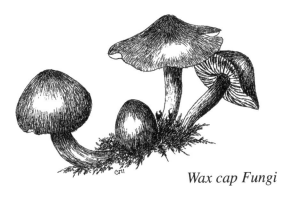

Wax cap Fungi

Practicals

Type of walk: A long walk mostly on tracks. The section on the old railway line, the Puggy Line, is wet in parts and involves crossing three ravines with burns in the bottom. This is easy in normal conditions but could be difficult, or impossible if the burns are in spate. Be prepared to turn back.

Distance: 10 miles / 16km
Time: 6–7 hours
Maps: OS Explorer 392 / Landranger 41

24

Dun Dearg
from Inverlair Bridge

Park by the stile into the plantation near to Inverlair Bridge, grid ref. 344807. The narrow road to the parking area leaves the A86 west of Tulloch Station.

By day a **woodcock** crouches in rough vegetation or in woodland, its colouring harmonising with its surroundings. At dusk its leaves

*River Spean
at Inverlair Bridge*

its 'hideaway' and sets off, flying low for a marshy area or ditch where it can use its downward pointing bill to probe for worms. Woodcocks have variable plumage, a wonderful combination of grey, chestnut, buff and black, in wavy lines or bars. On spring evenings they fly low over their woodland territories, making a curious noise that consists of a squeak and a grunt; this territorial marking behaviour is called 'roding'.

Walk 24

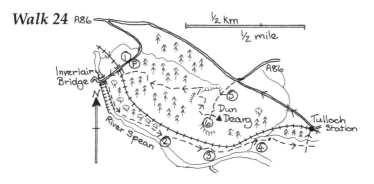

1 From the parking area, walk on down the lane. Cross the railway bridge and then stand on the next bridge to see the magnificent gorge through which, far below, flows the River Spean. Then return to take the ladder stile, now on your right, onto a wide grassy trod beside the gorge on your right and with conifers to your left. Carry on to pause where the river descends in twin waterfalls into the dramatic gorge. Stroll on the delightful way, soon to pass through birch woodland, where the river moves away, right. Below you, and to the right, is a side stream of the River Spean separated from the main flow by stones. Then you arrive at a fine fishing hut, with a picnic table close by, and a gate down to the side of the river. The tributary coming in opposite the hut is the Allt Laire.

2 Do not go through the gate but continue along inside the fence. After passing 20 posts and guiders, wind round left and climb uphill to an obscured way-marker post. Make sure you locate this post and do not try to progress through the dense conifers beside the burn. Then go on up over a great slab of rock, covered with moss, and wind right through the conifers on a distinct path. It soon leaves these trees and rises gently through bracken and birch. Continue on up a short rough slope and then follow the indistinct way where it descends to a gate.

3 Carry on, now outside the fence, with care, and then along the top of a wall, below the railway line, with a drop down to the shoreline of the river. Stride on to a gate and a ladderstile and, from the far side of the foot of the latter, walk on inside the fence. Cross a tiny stream and then a wet area to come to the side of the Allt Fhionnaghail. Step across on convenient stones, though if it is in spate, this might cause problems and you will have to return by your outward route.

4 Walk on uphill, left, through bracken to join a way-marked wide track, going right, and littered with pine needles. It then passes through larch. At a cross of tracks turn left. Continue on the ride to pass below spruce and carry on to a ladderstile to come to the edge of the railway track, with Tulloch station across the line and to your right. Go over the line with due care and wind right behind the station buildings, now an independent hostel. Join a minor road and walk left for ¼ mile / ½km to wind round a small telephone exchange. Just beyond it, on the left, climb the stile and follow the excellent reinforced path as it begins to climb up the long slope of Dun Dearg.

5 Follow the path as it winds left through heather and on up. At a small brow, turn left and climb up onto the top of the hill. The high flat area must have given the inhabitants a wonderful view of the surrounding area and was excellent for spotting attackers. From here you can see at least 8 Munros (mountains over 3000 ft).

6 Descend the little path and turn left. Almost immediately turn right as directed by the way-mark. Follow the path as it starts its descent, down a gully and then winding left and right to go round under the low crags at the foot of the dun. Continue on the path as it heads

Woodcock

92

towards the forest. Then follow it as it takes you along a ride, below Scots pine. Note the way-mark directing you right and then left. Continue gently descending on a long ride, where purple moor grass flourishes on either side, to arrive at the side of the railway line. Turn right to reach a fence. Here turn right again to walk the short distance to the stile where you have parked.

Bog Asphodel

Practicals

Type of walk: A lovely varied walk through coniferous and deciduous woodland, beside a fine river, across moorland and then a short climb to a dun.

Distance: 2 ½ miles / 4km
Time: 1 ½ hours
Maps: OS Explorer 393 / Landranger 41

25

Creag Pitridh

Park at the west end of Loch Laggan, grid ref. 433830. Here there is a concrete bridge over the River Spean and a large lay-by immediately east of the track to the bridge. At grid ref. 428983 (110 yds / 100m west) there is another lay-by if the first one is full. Access this by the A86 between Spean Bridge and Newtonmore.

Creag Pitridh is a fine neat rocky peak with significant cliffs on its north-western and eastern faces. At 3029 ft / 924m it is the lowest and most accessible of a group of three Munros south of Loch Laggan and on the northern edge of an area of wilderness and big mountains culminating in Ben Alder; an area which is not penetrated by any public roads. Any walk in this area is long but there is a good network of tracks and stalkers' paths. The estate is Ardverikie, now well-known as the location for much of the filming of the television series 'Monarch of the Glen'. Walkers are welcome but deer stalking does take place on the estate so please make enquiries about walking there between mid-August and the end of October, ring 01528 544300.

Lochan na-h-Earba

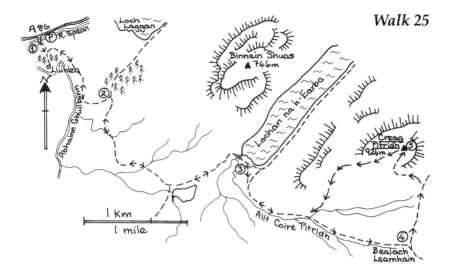

1 Walk down the track to the river and cross the concrete bridge, enjoying the fine views west to the Grey Corries and Stob Ban. Go through the gate beyond, where a notice welcomes walkers, and after 220 yds / 200m turn left at the edge of a small pinewood. Cross a deer fence by a high stile and follow the track as it swings round along the bank of the Abhainn Ghuilbinn, a wide river full of rapids. After a ½ mile / 1km the track swings away from the river and begins to climb gently.

2 Turn right at the next junction by another clump of pines and walk the pleasant track around the base of Binnein Shuas. Take the left turn just before a small lochan (reservoir) and follow the now level track to the end of Lochan na-h-Earba, where it swings right to cross a wooden bridge. There are sandy beaches here where you

Cloudberry

95

Osprey

may wish to linger and the view up the lochan is magnificent. Sandpipers bob and trill around the edges in spring and summer, and on any of these lochs you may spot black-throated divers.

3 Take the right fork at a Y-junction (the left fork is less distinct) and look for a grassy path to the right, its start marked by a small cairn. Follow this across the flats and on up beside a burn, the Allt Coire Pitridh, which forms a series of delightful small cascades. Cross a tributary burn on convenient stones and carry on up the clear stalkers' path. Beinn a'Chlachair towers on your right, whilst Creag Pitridh to your left looks small and neat! The path levels out in a wide pass, the Bealach Leamhain.

4 Look for another small cairn on the left marking another stalkers' path, which you should take. It rises gently to the col between Creag Pitridh and Geal Charn, the large sprawling mountain east of Creag Pitridh. At the high point of the col take a small clear path on the left, crossing the high morainy ground towards Creag Pitridh. This is where you are most likely to spot ptarmigan. Climb steeply up the rocky slope beyond the moraines; the crags are broken and the path winds easily through them, zig-zagging upwards. Soon it reaches a crest of rock and 110 yds / 100m further on is the summit cairn, perched on a knoll, from where there is a splendid view.

5 Leave the summit by a small path heading south-west. It is very clear down through rocky ground but eventually reaches a long grassy rake where it vanishes. At the bottom of the rake head in a westerly direction towards a long craggy ridge but turn south-west again before you reach it and descend the grassy heathery slopes towards the junction of a tributary burn (crossed on the way up) with the Allt Coire Pitridh. There are traces of a path on the bank of the tributary. Join the four mile-long stalkers' path by which you ascended and turn right. As you retrace your steps enjoy the wildlife of this remote area; in addition to divers and sandpipers you may see golden plover, dunlin and oystercatchers. Look for mergansers on the lochs and ospreys flying over and maybe fishing. In winter, of course, there will be much less to see, but there are always deer!

Ptarmigan

Practicals

Type of walk: This is a long but easy walk, mostly on tracks and stalkers' paths, to a fine small summit with excellent views, achieved with a minimum of steep climbing. It takes you into the fringes of a remote wilderness area and the wildlife is varied and plentiful at the right time of year.

Distance: 11 miles / 17km
Time: 6 hours
Maps: OS Explorer 393 / Landranger 42

26

Coire Ardair (Creag Meagaidh)

Parking: In the SNH car park just off the road near Aberarder Farm, grid ref. 483872. This is accessed from the A86 Spean Bridge to Newtonmore, about halfway along Loch Laggan.

Creag Meagaidh is a huge whaleback of a mountain straddling the Druim Alban, the spine of Scotland. To its west the River Roy drains towards the Great Glen and ultimately out into Loch Linnhe, and to its east rises the Spey which drains into the Moray Firth east of Inverness. Ice has carved the edges of the plateau into spectacular corries, two of which hold lochans. Ptarmigan and dotterel haunt the summit.

Creag Meagaidh **National Nature Reserve** was created by the Nature Conservancy Council (now SNH) in 1985 following an

Coire Ardair

outcry when the lower slopes were threatened with commercial afforestation. Deer numbers on the land have been significantly reduced, partly by catching the deer and selling them on to deer farms, and sheep have been excluded. As a result the birchwoods are regenerating, bringing an increase in their associated plants and wildlife. There are still deer on the reserve but they now form a manageable part of the ecosystem, not the dominant factor.

Coire Ardair is the most spectacular of several ice-gouged corries cut into the Creag Meagaidh massif. The splendid cliffs overlooking Lochan a'Choire are too vegetated for satisfactory summer rock-climbing but are said to be some of the best in Scotland for winter mountaineering.

Walk 26

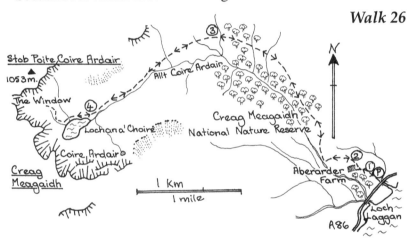

1 Go through the gap in the wall at the far end of the car park, where there is an information board for the reserve. Walk on up the track, which has wide verges supporting many flowering plants including melancholy thistles, with oak and birch woodland beyond. Here you might spot siskins flying overhead. On the right behind a deer fence is a small herd of red deer, kept to study numbers and effects on the vegetation. The track ends shortly at Aberarder Farm; take the right fork at the Y junction and pass to the right of the farm, past a small shelter with benches, tables and information about the reserve. Continue up the path behind the farm through a gap in the wall and past another information board. You are warned that sleepers, which make up parts of the path, can be very slippery when wet.

99

2 The path leads on up into the glen through scattered birch. All the wettest areas have sleeper paths, a small steep rise has been pitched, and some of the rest has been drained; further away from the farm it reverts to more ordinary rough stalkers' path apart from the sleepers over the bogs. It winds up onto the hillside well above the moraines and peaty hollows of the valley bottom. In places there are woods of mature birch, and a lot of regeneration is taking place, thanks to the substantial reduction in the number of deer. Primroses flower among the birches in spring, followed by cow-wheat and globeflowers, with heath spotted orchids and bog asphodel in the wet areas. Look for stonechats and meadow pipits beside the path, and ravens soaring overhead.

3 Follow the path as the glen curves round from north-west to south-

Red deer

west, becoming more enclosed. The long ridge to the north culminates in the Munro, Stob Poite Coire Ardair. As you come round the corner a steep sided glacial gap called The Window comes into view, then the fine cliffs of Creag Meagaidh which enclose the head of Coire Ardair. The path descends a little and runs above the burn, then climbs gently up through moraines and over a lip. In front is the lovely remote Lochan a'Choire, backed by the magnificent cliffs.

4 The path continues along the side of the lochan and then very steeply up moraine, scree and rocks into The Window, from where it is an easy climb onto either Creag Meagaidh or Stob Poite Coire Ardair. This walk however returns, after a suitable pause by the lochan, back down the glen by the path of ascent. Enjoy the views of Loch Laggan and the hills behind it as you come round the corner and descend to Aberarder Farm through the developing birch woodland.

Globe flowers

Practicals

Type of walk: Straightforward on clear paths all the way, with sleeper walkways over much of the bog. Take care over these in wet weather as they can be slippery.

Distance: 7 miles / 11.4km
Time: 3–4 hours
Maps: OS Explorer 401 / Landranger 34

NB No dogs. Walkers welcome at all times.

Bohuntine Hill
and Parallel Roads, Glen Roy

Park at the viewpoint in Glen Roy, grid ref. 298854. To reach this, leave the A86 at Roybridge and take the very dramatic, narrow road, with passing places, that runs through Glen Roy on the west side of the river.

The parallel roads, an ice-age monument, traverse the slopes all up Glen Roy, also in Glen Spean and parts of the Great Glen. For centuries it was claimed that they were made by the legendary Celtic giant, Fingal. Later they were believed to be man-made and they were called the 'King's Hunting roads'. Charles Darwin believed they were brought about by a marine phenomenon and only changed his mind after years of controversy. Parallel Roads or 'fossil' shorelines were created during the last glaciation, when the glen was dammed by a glacier and so filled with water to form a huge loch. As the glacier retreated and diminished, the water level sank and new shorelines formed. Today these are gravel ledges about 30 ft wide, sometimes with footpaths or animal tracks along them, which are barely a foot wide.

Parallel Roads, Glen Roy

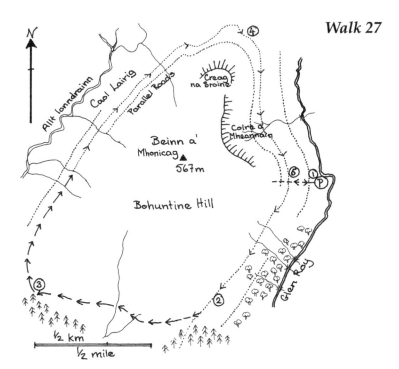

1 From the lovely high-level parking area, climb the slopes of Beinn a' Mhonicag to the first 'road' at about 860 ft / 260m. Continue up the delightful grassy sward to the second 'road' at approximately 1080 ft / 330m. Here turn left to walk a narrow path on the flat area of the 'road', through heather. Carry on along the path as it remains on the same contour, crossing several small burns that race down the hill slope, the 'road' disappearing as it intersects the burns. After rain take care as you traverse the path as it can become muddy especially where it comes close to the edge of the steep hill slope. Continue on to a fence, which you cross by a stile.

2 Beyond, follow the little path as it nears a plantation on the slopes of Meall Dubh. Do not enter the trees but begin to bear right up the pathless heather moorland, where you might flush out a snipe probing the ooze. Walk the higher ground, keeping parallel with, but well away from, a fence now on your left. Cross the Allt a Choileachain where an all terrain vehicle crosses and carry on along a poorly defined path. Soon you can see another plantation on your left and here you should keep about 160 ft / 50m above it, eventually winding down to the corner of the trees, where there is a piece of wooden fence that is easy to climb.

3 Beyond, slant down a little at first and then follow a path that heads right and remains on the same contour. Below, to your left, is the valley of Allt Coire Ionndrainn, the little burn meandering and sparkling as it goes, relieving some of the gloom of the conifer plantations that crowd its far bank. Soon you should pick up another 'road'. Eventually it begins to wind steadily round the shoulder of the hill, curving towards Glen Roy. Here you might disturb a woodcock. Ignore the peat path that drops down to the road through the valley and take the high level path through heather that remains on the same contour at approximately 330m.

4 Follow the path as it winds on round and passes through small grassy patches much favoured by the sheep. Then carry on along a 'road' as it curves round below crags in Coire a'Mheannain and continue until you reach the point where you started your walk.

Pause here to look across the River Roy to see the parallel 'roads' on the slopes of Leanna Mhor and also look back up Glen Roy to see more lines.

Snipe

5 Then begin your descent of the steepish slopes to the lower 'road'. Carry on down to the car park.

Practicals

Type of walk: Airy, open and challenging. You will not find any pitched paths or way-marks and sometimes the way is pathless, therefore remain roughly on the same contour, except where crossing the hill.

Distance: 7 miles / 11.2km
Time: 3–4 hours
Maps: OS Explorer 400 / Landranger 41 and on 34

Lower River Spean

Park outside the church and disused school at Kilmonivaig, grid ref. 212820. To access this from Spean Bridge take the A82 in the direction of Inverness. Just beyond the village turn left on to a small road, signposted 'Kilmonivaig Church and school'.

Both these two walks go to High Bridge, but on opposite sides of the River Spean. Each has a different parking place.

The High Bridge was constructed under the supervision of General Wade, to span the steep-sided Spean Gorge as a crucial link on his road to Inverness. The first stone was laid in 1736 but by the early 1800s the bridge was becoming unsafe. Today it is derelict, the pillars are crumbling and metal parts decayed.

The railway branch line from Spean Bridge to Inverness was opened in 1903. Passenger services were withdrawn in 1933. The line always made a loss. Far too much money was spent on elaborate viaducts and bridges. An extension to the pier at Fort Augustus was only open for three years.

Kilmonivaig Church

105

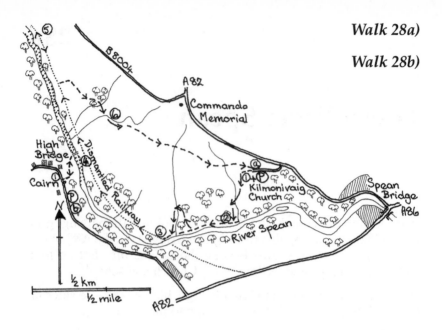

Walk 28a)

Walk 28b)

1 Walk beside the unoccupied school and schoolhouse and then down the grassy bank at the edge of the football field, to leave by a gate at the bottom. Turn left to follow the school fence to the corner. (If the buildings become used once more, there is a wooden gate at the right hand end of the fence by the car park which leads onto the open hill, and from here the school fence can be followed round to the other gate, and then to the corner.) Enjoy the magnificent view of the Grey Corries and the Nevis Range. At the end of the school fence, take a line downhill towards the River Spean. Pass under the power lines, turn right by the first electricity pole and pick the best line through a slightly boggy area until you reach a small burn. Cross this, then follow the burn down to a fishermen's path along the bank of River Spean, where you turn right.

2 Stroll through the beautiful oak woodland, with the turbulent river on your left. Follow the path as it becomes narrower and passes above a gorge. Then the oak trees give way to a more open area with rhododendron bushes and alders fringing the river. Follow the winding path through bracken under more mature oaks, with birch wood to the right. At a tributary stream take a small path, branching right into the birches a little before the gully. Find the best line through bracken and birch scrub until you reach the stream

106

at an easier crossing point higher up. Then follow its bank back to the fishermen's path along the Spean and carry on along this until the pier of the old railway bridge looms up in front. Turn right through the posts of the old railway fence, and follow a little path going steeply up the side of the railway embankment.

3 This railway was part of the branch line that originally was intended to run from Spean Bridge to Inverness, but it only reached Fort Augustus. The trackbed provides a splendid elevated greenway, high above the Spean Gorge. It is not recommended for adventurous children or unruly dogs. Where the Spean runs close to the trackbed, there are dramatic views down to the river. Carry on where the way swings away to the right and follow the track as it runs through a cutting. Here the ground is very boggy, but small paths have been made, always on the left side, neatly avoiding the bogs.

4 When a small cottage comes into view on the top of the opposite bank, you are approaching High Bridge. In summer, with leaves on the trees, it is impossible to get a good view of the remains of the bridge, just enticing glimpses, and the precipitous nature of the railway embankment and the gorge make adventurous exploration for the perfect view highly dangerous. A better view is possible from the other side, as described in walk b). Continue along the trackbed, which can be wet, but the gravel base is still present, so any puddles are not deep. Pass through another boggy cutting, walking on the left, and head on to an ancient wooden gate, which is quite easy to step over. Here the railway continues as an elevated route through more open country, with the magnificent River Spean a long way below. A bulldozed track leads up to the right, which is

Stonechat

the start of the return route, but a small extension of the walk along the railway is highly recommended for the fine views.

5 Eventually the track ends at a locked gate before a caravan park. Retrace your steps to the bulldozed track now leading up to your left. A very short distance up the field, this track meets an ancient grassy route. Turn right on this, go through a gate and on through birch woodland. Emerge from the trees on to open hillside, which in summer is covered with bracken. This makes route-finding difficult.

6 Head for a single large birch tree, from where the ancient trackway goes straight ahead. Cross two very small burns, then follow the turf dyke of an old settlement round to the left. Head for an oak tree and a larch side by side. Above to your left you can see the Commando Memorial on the skyline. Continue on the track over open hillside, with superb views of the mountains on your right, until the little Kilmonivaig church comes into view ahead. Aim for the far left corner of the parking area, where there is a wooden gate.

Wood Warbler

Practicals

Type of walk: Short but full of interest along a dramatic river gorge. The way can be wet in places, and care must be taken above the cliffs.

Distance: 3 miles / 5km
Time: 2 hours
Maps: OS Explorer 392 / Landranger 34 and 41—on both

High Bridge

Park in a very large passing place, on the right, just before the first house at Highbridge, leaving plenty of room for cars to pass, grid ref. 200820. To access this, take the A82 from Spean Bridge in the direction of Fort William and turn into the first right, signposted 'Highbridge, Brackletter and Kilmonivaig'. Follow this for almost a mile, cross a cattle grid and pass a sign advertising B&B at Highbridge.

The Spean is a big river, subject to sudden spates and flooding. So High Bridge made a huge improvement to travel from the north. In 1745 a small group of Jacobites ambushed a much larger number of Redcoats crossing the High Bridge on their way to reinforce the Garrison at Fort William. This was the first skirmish of the 1745 rebellion. A few yards on along the road from the parking area there is a memorial cairn beside the road, telling about the battle.

1 Just beyond the memorial, at the edge of the wooden fence of the first house, go down steps on the right, then along a gravel path with sections of boardwalk. This is well laid but a little used route down to the remains of the bridge. At the end of the last section of boardwalk, the old military road continues down to the right until a small fence prevents access on to the top of the bridge. To get the best view, go very carefully along a tiny path to the left, aware that below you are cliffs forming the gorge of the River Spean. The best time to see the dramatic crumbling remains of the bridge is in winter or spring, when there are no leaves on the trees. Retrace your steps up the track to the boardwalk and back to your car.

Practicals

Type of walk: Very short easy walk mainly to see the remains of the High Bridge. See map on page 106.

Distance: ½ mile / 1k
Time: ½ hour
Maps: OS Explorer 392 / Landranger 34 and 41—on both

29

Loch Lochy and Achnacarry

Park at Gairlochy, grid ref. 183850. To reach this turn off north of Spean Bridge onto the B8004 just beyond the Commando Memorial and descend to Gairlochy and the Caledonian Canal. Cross the swing bridge, and bear right. At the top of the slope keep right again and park in the large lay-by, on the right, 850 yds / 800m along the road from the junction.

British Waterways Scotland wants people to make full use of the Caledonian Canal for recreation. They achieve this by working with others wanting to encourage visitors to benefit from the outstanding scenery of the Great Glen. Along many stretches, the towpath beside the canal provides a route for both the Great Glen Mountain Bike Trail, set up first, and then the Great Glen Way a long distance footpath that uses many forestry tracks as well as the Canal bank.

Clan Cameron Museum

1 Descend from the parking area, following the Great Glen Way, a designated long distance walk, that winds left to continue beside Loch Lochy. This lovely way leads through conifers and then into fine deciduous woodland. Cross a sturdy footbridge and pass below beech and oak, both magnificent in autumn. As the loch is part of the route from the west coast to the east coast, watch as you go the various craft, such as trawlers and yachts, which use this short cut to avoid the much longer and arduous route through the Pentland Firth.

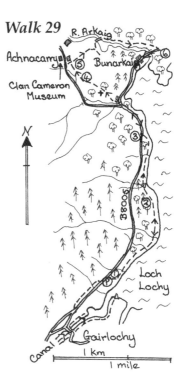

Walk 29

2 Go on through more conifers as the path moves away from the loch. Then cross a footbridge over a pretty burn and follow the track as it winds right and soon comes beside the loch once more. Stroll on with the lovely sheet of water to your right and with Meall nan Teanga ahead. Conifers come right up to the left side of the footpath, their gloom sometimes relieved by a tree creeper assiduously ascending the tree trunks, probing for prey. Go on to cross two more footbridges over burns, rushing to deposit their water in the loch. Here in the shallows you might spot a dipper running, under water, searching for its next meal. Carry on along the path as it moves out into scattered birch, oak and bracken as the way continues parallel with the narrow road. Watch here for goldcrests and long tailed tits, and also cormorants flying up the loch.

3 Stride the path to join the minor road and walk on towards the tiny hamlet of Bunarkaig. Go past the ornate gates through which passes a narrow lane to Achnacarry. Stroll on over the next bridge and go past one house. Before the next house, a sign directs you left, up a track, to St Ciaran's Church. Follow the track as it climbs steadily to pass through a deer gate and arrive in front of the austere church set among deciduous woodland. Then carry on along the pleasing

111

Brambling

track, which can be wet in winter. Continue on to pass on your left, a row of fine young beech.

4 Cross a footbridge and walk on to take a deer gate on the left. Strike across the pasture to join a track that runs beside a cottage, opposite to the Clan Cameron Museum, with its cannon outside. Ahead is a fine view of Achnacarry House, home of Cameron of Locheil, the clan Chieftain. It was used for commando training and accommodation during the war, hence the memorial.

5 Return to the track beside the cottage and, ignoring where you joined it, continue along the delightful fenced way, with Achnacarry House to your left. Wind right, leaving the old walled garden of the laird's house to your left, to go through a deer gate. Bear round

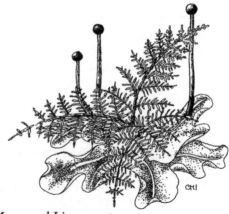

Feather Moss and Liverwort

112

left to walk beside the deer-fenced woodland to your left, with the River Arkaig to your right. Stroll on to cross the footbridge over the surging water and bear slightly right to head on along a grassy, narrow path through dense rhododendrons. To your right, the sound deadened slightly by the bushes, you can hear the river descending, tumultuously, over its rocky bed. Carry on the narrow path until you reach the road at Bunarkaig.

6 Turn right and cross the bridge over the river and walk on until you reach the path, on your left, taken earlier. Retrace your steps through the pleasing woodland.

NB Before you leave this gloriously peaceful area you may like to descend from the parking area by turning left at the first road junction and then left again to the side of the Caledonian Canal. Cross the swing bridge and walk left along the towpath to the double set of locks where the canal leaves Loch Lochy. Pause here to look at the large basin just beyond, where colourful boats tie up and where you might spot a kingfisher. Then cross the lock bridge and walk back along the opposite bank. Turn right at the road and then right again to climb the hill to the parking area.

Kingfisher

Practicals

Type of walk: Charming walk on generally level paths, tracks and narrow almost traffic-free roads.

Distance: 6 miles / 9.5km
Time: 3–4 hours
Maps: OS Explorers 400, 399 (on both) / Landrangers 41, 34 (on both)

30

Loch Arkaig and Invermallie

Park in the superb car park close to the Chia-Aig Falls, grid ref. 176888. To reach this take the A82 for ten miles, north, from Fort William, until just past the Commando Memorial. Turn left along the B8004 to cross the Caledonian Canal at Gairlochy. Wind right to continue on the B8005 for 5 miles to reach the car park, on the right.

End of Loch Arkaig

Ponies or garrons

This walk takes you along the south side of **Loch Arkaig**, which lies in one of the least spoiled valleys in the Highlands. The long track is edged with deciduous trees where you will hear only the gentle lapping of the water on the shore and bird song. After 1 ¾ miles / 3km a grassy trod leads off, right, from the newly made continuing track. The old track leads across grassy flats to a bothy, a six roomed cottage. Behind it flows a shallow burn, River Mallie, hurrying to join the loch. Beyond the river are pastures where sturdy horses graze. Take care here because they wade the stream, intent on grazing on your sandwiches.

The **falls of Chia-Aig** are dramatic. The little river above, in enormous haste to join Loch Arkaig, hurtles down the steep hillside in two magnificent falls. The lower one descends into a seething plunge pool known as the Witch's Cauldron. The legend behind its name is that when the cattle of the area fell sick, the Camerons consulted a seer who suggested that an old woman, who lived beside the loch, was the cause. He said that only when she was dead would the cattle get better. So the men visited her cottage and found just a cat, which they fell upon and wounded. The cat escaped as best it could, leaving a trail of blood that led to the pool. The men followed the trail and as they approached the cat, by the pool, it let out a terrifying scream and changed into the witch. The Camerons stoned her to death and the cattle got better.

115

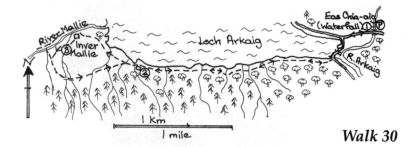

1 Turn right out of the car park and walk to the bridge over the Witch's Cauldron, where you will want to pause. Stroll on and take the first left, a private road, where walkers are welcome, to walk beside Loch Arkaig to your right and the Abhainn Chia-Aig to your left. Cross a small bridge and then a short distance along cross the long white bridge where water surges out of loch and continues as the River Arkaig. Wind right to pass round a barrier to join a wide track that passes through glorious mixed woodland, with the loch to your right. Here you might spot common snipe and heron. Carry on the roller-coaster way, with deciduous trees lining the track and follow it as it moves away from the loch through birch woodland. Then the track descends again and comes closer to the shore, where from the trees come the gentle calls of bullfinches.

2 Continue past a cottage, on the left, and through a sturdy wall. Cross a small, shallow ford and then look for the easy-to-miss grassy track leaving, right, from the continuing newly made track (new at the time of writing). Head on through a small copse and then move out into open boggy grassland, with the lake to your right. The reinforced old track is most pleasing. Look up into the tops of

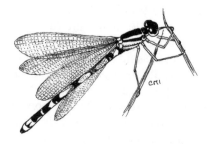

Common blue damselfly

scattered trees, on your right, where you might spot siskins and on the scattered bushes, to your left, for stonechats. Then press on to the bothy. Here on the stony low wall, in the sun, might be the place for your picnic.

3 Stride on along the track to ford the burn hurrying down from Glen Mallie, chattering as it goes, to join the loch. If the burn is in spate and impassable, return by your outward route. Once across the burn, follow a track, left, to join the newly constructed track. Go on left along it and wind left as it heads back to the cottage in the wood. Carry on along your outward route to return to the car park.

Bullfinches

Practicals

Type of walk: A good track all the way beside Loch Arkaig to a bothy out in pastures. One burn to ford.

Distance: 6 miles / 9.5km
Time: 3–4 hours
Maps: OS Explorer 399 / Landranger 34 or 41 (on both)

31

Glen Dessarry

Park at the road end, grid ref. 988916, where there is a barrier to prevent unauthorised vehicles from going further. There is room for about 8 cars in various spaces on the verges but please do not obstruct the turning space. To access this, drive along the very narrow switchback road from Gairlochy, west of Spean Bridge. The road goes all along the side of Loch Arkaig and is very beautiful—if you are not driving!

Knoydart is one of the most wild and inaccessible areas of Scotland. The path along which this walk returns through **Glen Dessarry** is part of a long right of way which crosses two mountain passes and eventually leads to Inverie, the only significant settlement in Knoydart. Even Inverie can only be reached by boat or on foot.

Glen Dessarry

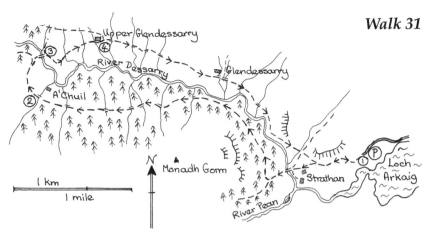

1 Go round the barrier and continue along the reinforced track. Admire the view across the valley towards Streap and Sgurr Thuilm at the far side of Glen Pean. Take the left branch at the next junction and walk down towards the river with the cottage of Strathan to your left. Cross the River Dessarry on a wide sturdy bridge and enter the forest by a stile over the deer fence, still heading towards Glen Pean. At a junction ¼ mile / ½ km further on, take the right branch which curves round and climbs gently, bringing you back into Glen Dessarry. Although this track is through forest there are wide open areas on both sides and many unforested spaces, so you do not feel enclosed and the views across Glen Dessarry are splendid. In autumn the hills are tawny with purple moor grass and the scattered birches stand out golden against the dark conifers; and the sound of stags roaring accompanies you all the way up the glen. Sgurr nan Coireachan comes into view on your right, looking very high, and at the head of the glen the pointed Bidein a' Chabair appears. Look along the skyline from time to time as you go; this is golden eagle country.

2 Go through an open derelict gate at the end of the forest and head downhill on the pleasant track, curving round towards the next block of forest. Just before the track reaches the gate into the trees, there is a wide turning space on the right. Take a small path which leaves the track at the back of this space. It goes down a bank and across a boggy area, crossing a tiny burn by a plank bridge, and on to the bank of the River Dessarry. Cross the good wooden footbridge. The River Dessarry is lovely here, with deep pools and shallow falls and rapids.

119

3 Beyond the bridge bear right and make for the edge of the steep ground (the path is not obvious). Go down onto the river flats and here you will find the path again, along the edge of a bog with the steep river terrace to

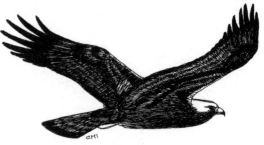

Golden Eagle

your left. Follow this path round to Upper Glendessarry cottage.

4 In front of the cottage, which is whitewashed and well-cared for, join a landrover track continuing back down the glen. This takes you past Glendessarry Lodge, now a heap of rubble plus some sheds, and on beside the delightful river, which is steeply below you and foams over little falls. As you round the corner of the glen, Streap and Sgurr Thuilm come into view again. Ignore a track down to your right and a right-of-way footpath to your left and rejoin the track coming up from Strathan, which you follow back to your car.

Practicals

Type of walk: A fairly level walk, mostly along good tracks with only one uncertain bit in the middle. It is an easy walk in the middle of one of the really wild areas of Scotland—the Rough Bounds of Knoydart. The mountain scenery is splendid. The only disadvantage (if it is one!) is that it is a very long way from anywhere at all and the cottages are not lived in all year round. Go well prepared.

Distance: 7 miles / 11.2km
Time: 4 hours
Maps: OS Explorer 398 / Landranger 33

NB Stalking takes place in this area from August 10th to October 10th. During this time you are asked to keep to the rights-of-way and paths marked on a map shown at the end of the road. The walk above is shown on the map and is acceptable all year round. There is no stalking on Sundays.

32

Caledonian Canal: Laggan Locks

Park in the car park for the Laggan Locks, grid ref. 287963. Approaching from the north, watch for the signpost for the locks, on the right, just after a bend on the A82, south of South Laggan. From the south it's on the left at the end of Loch Lochy.

Close by the car park, at the foot of Loch Lochy, was the site of the **Battle of the Shirts**. Here several hundred Frasers and even

The Eagle *Laggan Locks*

more MacDonalds and Camerons fought to the death. The July day was very warm and the clansmen found it too hot to fight in their heavy woollen plaids (kilts). So they removed them and fought in their long shirts. All day the battle raged and hundreds died; only a dozen clansmen walked away.

In 1903 the **Fort William to Fort Augustus railway** was constructed. It terminated at the pier at Fort Augustus for passengers to join the Loch Ness passenger steamers to Inverness. The line was never a commercial success and had proved very expensive to build. It was closed to passenger services in 1933.

Walk 32

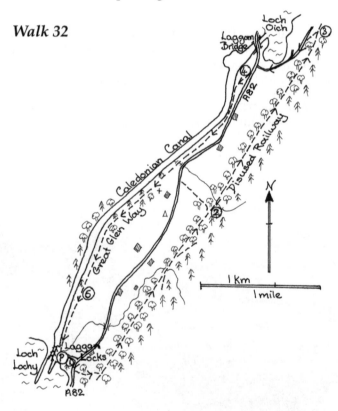

1 Walk the access track to return to the A82. Cross with care and, a short distance to the right, go ahead into an a grassy lay-by and then up a path that is not very obvious at first but very soon becomes most pleasing. At the top of the slope, turn left onto a forestry track, once the old railway line that was traversed for a short distance in walk 33. Stroll on along the way, which is lined with deciduous trees. The verges support lush low-level vegetation, colourful with an array of flowers at the right time of the year. After a mile, the track swings left to join the A-road.

2 This walk continues on along the old railway line, now just a reinforced path, muddy in parts, passing through even more lush vegetation. Enjoy the several streams that are channelled under the trackbed. Pause where the track crosses the Allt na Lagain and look up to see a series of fine waterfalls descending through the conifers above. Continue beneath hazels where they form an arch overhead, no longer cut back for the trains. Look for roe deer. Then the way opens out and here you can spot traces of the old station of Laggan. Descend a few steps left to join the Great Glen Way.

3 Turn left and walk the minor road that leads to the Great Glen Water Park and turn left. Pass Station House (passed in the opposite direction in walk 33), and carry on. As you go notice the fen on either side and a pleasing glimpse of the foot of Loch Oich. Cross the A82 and a couple of steps, left, take the way-marked path along the Great Glen Way to walk a reinforced track, gradually moving away from the noisy A-road.

4 Look for the pretty climbing corydalis trailing over the bushes. Pass through a large area of gorse and more corydalis. And then you can look down on the Caledonian Canal. Here it does not appear

Roe deer

123

a bit like a canal. It is in fact a glorious river that flows through lofty deciduous trees, crowding both banks, and with no towpath. Then the good path, sometimes a track, takes you beneath magnificent redwoods, with glimpses of the canal down through the trunks.

5 Eventually the path descends and comes to a wide grassy area beside the canal. Walk on to view the Laggan Locks and then turn left to return to the car park.

Bogbean

Practicals

Type of walk: A charming short walk just right for a sunny summer evening or for the first day of your walking holiday.

Distance: 4 miles / 6.5km
Time: 2 hours
Maps: OS Explorer 400 / Landranger 34

Loch Oich circular

Park at Oich Bridge, grid ref. 338036. To access this travel along the A82, north-east from Invergarry, and turn left before the Aberchalder swing bridge over the Caledonian Canal that links Loch Oich with Loch Ness.

Close by the parking area is the elegant **Oich Bridge**. In 1849 floods swept through the Great Glen breaching the Caledonian Canal and destroying the stone bridge over the River Oich. It took five years to replace the latter with a double cantilever bridge, designed by engineer James Dredge. Each half of the bridge can support its own weight at the end of each cantilever. The middle of the bridge, therefore, has little weight and needs no support. The river needed a single wide span to avoid the danger of more floods so a stone bridge was out of the question. You can admire the bridge and cross it but you can not walk beyond as the Aberchalder estate does not allow access; the gate is locked.

Bridge of Oich

1 From the parking area return to the A82 and walk right along the pavement to pass another car park, which you might need to use if the small one by the canal is full. Wind round the bend and take the signposted 'Great Glen Cycle Route', on the right, where you climb steadily for a short distance

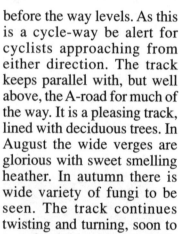

Walk 33

before the way levels. As this is a cycle-way be alert for cyclists approaching from either direction. The track keeps parallel with, but well above, the A-road for much of the way. It is a pleasing track, lined with deciduous trees. In August the wide verges are glorious with sweet smelling heather. In autumn there is wide variety of fungi to be seen. The track continues twisting and turning, soon to wind sharply right and descending to a footbridge over the Allt Leth-bheinne.

2 Carry on the pleasant way, ignoring the narrow left turn through the conifers to Drynachan. Walk on and then follow the track as it descends towards the A82. Turn right on the wide cycle track, following a large red arrow painted on a boulder, and walk on to where the track swings sharp right. Here go on ahead (left) as directed by a signboard for the cycle route. As you stroll the delightful shelf-like way look for speckled wood butterflies, flitting

126

from plant to plant. Ahead enjoy the panoramic view of the hills across Glen Garry, which is dominated by Ben Tee (2950 ft / 901m) and Sron a' Choire Ghairbh (the nose of the rough corrie) (3180 ft / 973m).

3 Watch for a small flat stone embedded in the path, with a painted white arrow, that directs you right. Carry on the way, which now continues as a path, as it zig-zags down the steep side of the hill and descends to the A87. Cross and walk right. Pass Glengarry Church on the opposite side of the road. Just beyond, take an unsigned track going off left. At the division of the way, take the left branch and follow it as it winds right, through trees, to come to the side of the River Garry. Walk on along the clear path, with the surging river to your left and houses to your right. And then the latter cease and the delightful path continues through woodland to come to a bridge over the wide river. Cross and go through a kissing gate. Wind right, over a small wooden bridge, and go on through a gate. Turn left and walk up beside the fence, over a wide pasture, with woodland surrounding this delightful meadow land. Go through a gate to join a narrow road.

4 Turn left and walk on for a few steps to cross a cattle grid and take, on the right, a signed cycle route. Climb gently along the good track. As you continue notice the large patches of Gaultheria, with tiny pendulous bell-shaped flowers, that colonise the steep sides of the verges (see walk 9). Ignore any side turns and head on gently climbing to where the path levels. Pause in a high grassy lay-by, on the left, for a magical view of Loch Oich. Look for Invergarry Castle Hotel. Closer and nearer the loch stand the ruins of Invergarry Castle. Stroll on along the terraced track to come to a hairpin bend. Here keep to the left fork to start your descent to the A82.

Fly Agaric and Ink Caps

127

5 At the A-road, turn right to walk the pavement. Where it runs out, cross and continue on the opposite side to walk a path, along the verge, to the Laggan swing bridge over the Caledonian Canal. Cross, using the pedestrian path, and at its end go through an iron gate on the left to join a road. Wind right and then left along a side road. As you continue enjoy the water meadows on either side, colourful with meadow sweet, valerian and bog bean in the wetter patches. Pass 'Station House' on the left (see walk 32) and then take, on the right, the way-marked track, the Great Glen Way, which runs along an old railway trackbed that once ran from Spean Bridge to Fort Augustus. This keeps well above Loch Oich at first. Then, eventually, follow the way-mark that directs you left and down a short slope to walk along the edge of the fine loch. This track is a surviving section of a General Wade Road.

6 Go through a large deer gate to continue. Across the loch you can see Invergarry Castle and then the hotel, viewed earlier. Go past a boarded up cottage, with a red roof and a blue painted porch, where there is a seat to enjoy the grand view. Then climb the sloping path to look over a fence to see the entrance to a tunnel, more of the old railway line. At the Aberchalder estate gated road, turn left and walk to the foot of steps, which you climb onto an old railway bridge over a tributary burn heading for Loch Oich. At the end of the bridge, turn sharp left through a way-marked kissing gate in a deer fence to saunter on along a lovely narrow grassy path. Follow the way-marks, right, to come beside the loch once more. Wind right and continue until you can climb a ladderstile to walk the fine turf beside the Caledonian Canal. At the Aberchalder swing bridge, cross by the pedestrian bridge and then cross the A-road to return to the parking area.

Practicals

Type of walk: This is an almost level route that is easy to walk. It takes you on forestry tracks, a disused railway track and part of an old military road.

Distance: 10 ½ miles / 16.5m
Time: 5–6 hours
Maps: OS Explorer 400 / Landranger 34

Allt na Cailliche Waterfalls, Glen Garry

Park in the Forestry Commission's car park at White Bridge, grid ref. 283013. To reach this leave the A87 two miles west of Invergarry and then follow signs down to the bridge, cross and turn right into the first car park.

River Garry is an exciting short stretch of river, full of rocks and rapids, between the dam at the end of Loch Garry and Loch Oich in the Great Glen. Once a week the sluices are opened on the Loch Garry Dam to keep the river in good condition and allow the salmon to come up. On 'dam release day', or after heavy rain, the river is particularly spectacular. Then it is very popular for white water kayaking.

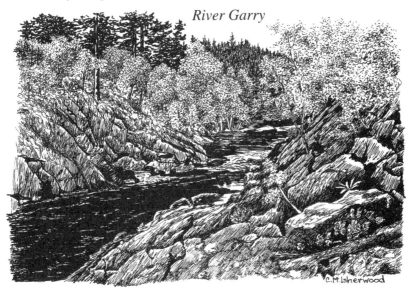

River Garry

1 Walk back to the bridge but do not cross; instead take the small path on the right, which goes along the river bank past a series of rapids and pools. Keep a lookout for dippers and grey wagtails. The path keeps close to the river and at one place runs along a raised bank with a deep ditch on the other side, possibly an old mill leat.

2 When the path reaches a substantial burn, the Allt na Cailliche, do not cross the somewhat ricketty bridge ahead but turn right up the way-marked path by the burn. This soon emerges into a turning circle for a forestry track. Here walk straight ahead to a T-junction with another forest track, where you should turn left. Continue on this track through another car park and a short distance beyond it turn left, signed by a yellow way-mark, to cross a concrete bridge over the Allt na Cailliche. Go past a cottage on the right, Forest Gate Cottage, and follow the track over another bridge. The way now becomes a surfaced road, contouring the hillside above the river, passing through deciduous trees, mainly beech and birch.

3 Take the first right turn, which is at an acute angle and goes back above Forest Gate Cottage. Climb gently to go through a wicket gate beside a deer gate and carry on uphill. The forest has been felled here and is regenerating, so the views are open. In autumn flocks of fieldfares descend on the rowans and strip their berries. As you climb, the shapely Beinn Tee comes into view ahead. Cross two burns by concrete bridges and after the second (the Allt na

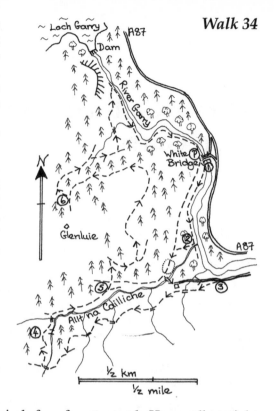

Cailliche again) take a small yellow way-marked path on the right which goes downhill beside it. The path curves away from the burn to pass through spruce underlaid with hummocks of feather moss and occasional hard ferns, then an open area with a fine 'granny' pine (see walk 35).

4 Descend a steep bank by steps, with the sound of waterfalls nearby on the right. There is a small enclosure with seats but the waterfall is not really visible from here. The well-made path comes into more level woodland. Here take the way-marked path on the right, which brings you to a fine viewpoint at the bottom of a splendid series of waterfalls. You will want to linger to admire them. Continue on the path, which goes along the lip of a small gorge, through birch woodland. You may see foraging parties of tits, blue, great, coal and long-tailed, and with them goldcrests and tree-creepers. Cross a bridge over a tributary burn and turn right at a T-junction.

5 After 55 yds / 50m, turn left at the red way-mark and climb up to a nearby forest track. Cross and follow a small path on the far side, up through a gate in a deer fence. Ascend steeply through open larch woodland to the top of a bank, where the path bears right and begins to contour, becoming a delectable mossy way under the arching larches. All too soon this ends at a hairpin bend on a forest track. Turn left and take the upper branch of the track (not way-marked). The track is fairly level and runs along the hillside with mature open spruce to the right and young mixed regenerating forest on the left. Ignore a path on the right with a green way-mark and continue on the track as it curves left until you reach an old quarry.

Fieldfare

6 Take the green way-marked track, which goes off on the right opposite the quarry. The track is old and grassy and passes through open scrubby trees with a small burn on the right. Where it continues as a very overgrown ride through older trees, leave it, right, following way-marks, along a raised bank through gorse. Then take the way-marked path on the left down through spruce. Cross a small bridge and descend steps to another grassy ride. Turn left and carry on through a narrow valley to a deer fence. Go through the gate and turn right; you are now back on the bank of the River Garry. Climb steeply to a fine viewpoint and then on down the far side. Enjoy the rapids and the churning waterfalls where the river foams and swirls through a rocky gorge. The path goes on round a wide bend under fine old oak and beech trees, eventually returning you to the car park.

Pine marten

Practicals

Type of walk: Interesting and varied, with some spectacular river scenery. All on paths and forest tracks. Fairly easy going.

Distance: 4 ½ miles / 7.4km
Time: 3 hours
Maps: OS Explorer 400 / Landranger 34

35

Glengarry:
Greenfield and Laddie Burn

Park just before the bridge over the narrow part of Loch Garry, grid ref. 195022. To access this drive west along the A87 for 5 ½ miles. Then turn left onto a minor road, signed to Kinlochourn and drive on for 3 ½ miles. Here take a single track lane, on the left, signposted Tornacarry, where there are also several right-of-way signs on the post. A short distance along and you reach a layby by the bridge. If the space is full, carry on over the bridge to park in one of several lay-bys along the continuing lane.

Since 1995 Forest Enterprise has embarked on a programme of harvesting non-native conifers to **reinstate the native pinewoods** to their former glory. On the right of the path, as you climb beside the Laddie burn, are a number of large 'granny' pines, some of which could be over 200 years old. They shed seed and in a good

*Waterfall
on Laddie Burn*

133

year, when conditions are ideal, the seeds germinate and, taking less than five years, develop into young saplings. At Greenfield, the old woods were used for hunting red deer by the MacDonnell clan who were keen and skilful deerstalkers. Settlements here in Glengarry were abandoned in the late eighteenth and early nineteenth century when higher rents and clearances for sheep forced whole families to emigrate to Canada.

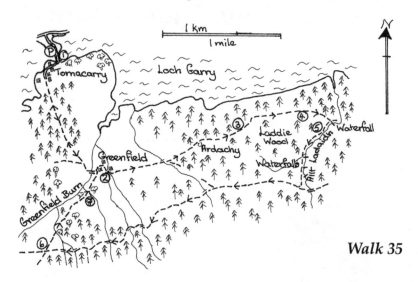

Walk 35

1 Cross the road bridge and walk on along the continuing narrow lane. Go past three houses at Tornacarry. Carry on through conifer and then birch woodland and, after a mile, cross a footbridge over the Greenfield Burn. At the Y-junction, in the hamlet of Greenfield, take the left branch and carry on past a cottage on either side of the way.

2 Walk on the rising reinforced track with another cottage on the left and outbuildings to the right. Cross, by a flat concrete bridge, the junction of two little streams. Go on climbing steadily through open ground where the forest has been cleared and scattered birch thrives. Pass through a gate in the deer fence. Look for sneezewort growing along the verge of the track. At the Y-junction, just before a conifer plantation, take the left branch to walk along the side of the forest. Then the track moves into the trees with wide colourful verges of moss, lichen and wild flowers.

134

3 Climb the low locked gate but pause here first to enjoy the glorious view ahead of scattered Caledonian pines and the ridge of hills beyond. Once over the gate, descend gently, with glimpses of Loch Garry below, to the left. Walk on until the wide track suddenly ceases to exist. Here take an unsigned rough path to descend a few steps, left, to an unsigned hurdle gate, which you need to lift off its housing to pass through.

4 Walk on along a narrow grassy footpath, with a drainage ditch on either side. After rain the path can be muddy in places and the tall vegetation rather wet. The path carries on beside a plantation, to the left, and scattered pines, to the right. Look for the occasional 'granny' pine and also dead ones that suffered during a fire in 1942. Continue on to reach the side of the Laddie Burn. To see one of its magnificent falls, turn left and walk on a few steps on a narrow path, high above the burn, as it plummets through rowan, alder, birch and larch. After viewing with care, return along the path and continue up the edge of the ravine.

5 This is a spectacular part of the walk. The Laddie descends in tumultuous cascades and several more dramatic falls as it thunders on its way to join Loch Garry. Eventually the path, and the burn, level out and the path moves away, right, to join a forest road, where you walk on right, with fine views over Glen Garry. Beyond a cattle grid you might come upon Highland cattle grazing. After the next cattle grid they are left behind. When the forest ceases on

Crested tit

the left (2 ¼ miles / 3.5km from where you joined the track), pause and look right to see an indistinct path, coming up from the direction of Greenfield. Its route continues across the forest road and heads for the hills.

6 Here turn acute right to follow the narrow path obliquely across open ground. After rain the path can be wet as it leads you gently to the edge of birch woodland. Cross a narrow stream, the Allt Giubhais, either at the ford or a little higher up on stones. A generally good path carries on, gradually descending through spruce on the left and larch to the right. Emerge from the trees and walk ahead to an electrified spring across the continuing grassy track. To pass through, use the insulated handle on the end of the spring to unhook it, pass through and re-hook it. Beyond walk the track as it winds downhill and then passes into birch woodland. The grassy way comes close beside a steam on your right as it descends to a ford over the Allt nan Corp (the burn of the corpses).

7 Cross this on boulders and climb ahead out of the trees to cross a boggy patch, where a bit of hopping from tuft to tuft is required after a rainy spell. The path is indistinct here but carry on, keeping to birch-clad higher ground. A better path soon emerges. Carry on out of the trees to go through a gate. Beyond it the path ends. Move across a wet patch, left, to pick up a wide grassy track that takes you past a cottage, on your right, at Greenfield. Go through a gate and join the cottage's access track. Wind round left and walk on to go over the bridge across the Greenfield Burn taken almost at the outset of the walk. Stroll back along the narrow lane to cross the bridge over the 'waist' of Loch Garry to reach the parking area.

Practicals

Type of walk: This is a pleasing walk on forest tracks and a narrow path beside a dramatic tumbling burn. The return path to Greenfield is a delight though perhaps a spirit of adventure is required. There is much to enjoy in this most beautiful glen.

Distance: 8 miles / 13km
Time: 4 hours
Maps: OS Explorer 400 / Landranger 34

36

Gleouraich
and Spidean Mialach

Park opposite the start of the path, grid ref. 028030. To access this turn left off the A87 4 ¼ miles / 7 km west of Invergarry onto the minor road to Kinlochhourn. Enjoy the beautiful drive along the shore of Loch Garry and then up the glen to the Loch Quoich dam. The walk starts part way along the north shore of Loch Quoich.

Gleouraich and Spidean Mialach are generally reckoned to be among the easiest climbs in the Western Highlands, because of their accessibility and the superb stalkers' paths. It is believed that the paths were constructed by the landowner's staff in anticipation of a visit from the king; unfortunately for him the king didn't come but the legacy of the paths is now a wonderful bonus for walkers. In spite of the ease with which they can be climbed they are splendid mountains, combining dramatic dark rocky corries on the northern

Loch Quoich and Sgurr na Ciche

137

side with gentler grassy slopes to the south. There are wonderful views across half of Scotland, to Ben Nevis in the south and Creag Meagaidh in the east and the incomparable Knoydart hills to south and west.

Loch Quoich is a hydro-electric loch and so in spite of its magnificent setting it sometimes has ugly draw-down lines around its shores. There is a large dam at the east-end beside the road up Glen Garry, and two small ones at the west in the wilderness area at the head of the Carnach River. The long arm of the loch extending north below the outflung ridge of Gleouraich is a result of the rise in water level, as are several drowned paths.

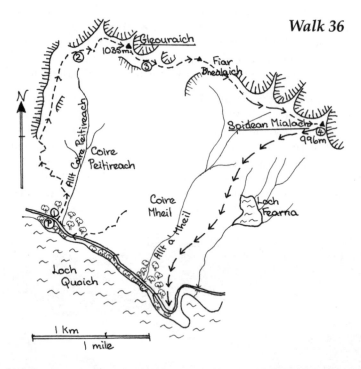

Walk 36

1 Leave the road by a small cairn just west of a burn, the Allt Coire Peitireach. The continuing path through gorse, rhododendron and birch scrub is passable but not very obvious. Shortly it emerges into the open and from now on it is a superb stalkers' path. Follow it up the line of the burn and then out onto the steep open hillside where it zig-zags gently upwards to ease the gradient. Eventually

Ring ousel

it gains the summit of a narrow ridge, Sron a'Chuilinn, with a vertiginous drop down to the narrow arm of Loch Quoich to the left and an equally steep but shorter drop to Coire Peitireach to the right. The path, however, continues to be excellent and there is no difficulty even in this airy situation. Turn round, occasionally, to admire the magnificent view back over Loch Quoich to the hills of the rough bounds of Knoydart, dominated by the lop-sided cone of Sgurr na Ciche.

2 Towards the end of the ridge the path drops down into a little hollow and then climbs again onto the side of Gleouraich proper. Here it ends at a pony stance; however a clear walkers' path continues up the edge of the hill to the summit ridge, not too far above. Walk along the ridge to your right, admiring the fine corries cut into the northern slopes of the mountain and the view across to the next range of hills, the South Kintail (or Cluanie) Ridge, seven Munros in a row. The summit of this Munro is soon gained. Here you can decide whether to retrace your steps, with the wonderful view across Loch Quoich in front of you, or, if feeling fit, whether to continue to the next Munro, Spidean Mialach.

3 If you decide to carry on, you are rewarded with a fine ridge walk along the edge of the northern corries to a top, Craig Coire na Fiar Bhealaich, where you pick up another stalkers' path which zig-zags down into the Fiar Bhealach below. Then climb steeply (and quite a long way) up slopes of short grass to the next top, and on

round the edge of two more splendid corries to the summit of Spidean Mialach. Listen for ring ousels singing in the corries below you, and watch out for a soaring eagle. The view along Loch Quoich from here is possibly even better than it is from Gleouraich.

4 Leave the summit, heading in a south-westerly direction and aiming to the right of a small lochan, Loch Fearna, which you can see well below you. Do not head down into the corrie but continue along the broad ridge on the west side of the loch all the way down to the road. Turn right to return to your car.

Crowberry and Bearberry

Practicals

Type of walk: Gleouraich and Spidean Mialach are considered easy Munros to climb because of the excellent stalkers' paths but they are very high hills and all the usual precautions should be taken, with full walking equipment.

Distance: 10 miles / 16km
Time: 6–7 hours
Maps: OS Explorer 414 / Landranger 33

NB: Stalking takes place from September 1st to October 10th and you are asked to avoid this walk during that time. The estate is Wester Glenquoich, tel. 01809 511 220. Keep to signed routes at all other times.

37

Kinloch Hourn to Barrisdale

Park near the road end in one of two good car parks, grid ref. 949066. One is a long-stay and the other a day one. There is a nominal fee of 50p. To access this take the minor road which leaves the A87, six miles west of Invergarry, signed Tomdoun and Kinlochhourn. It is 26 miles / 42km to Kinlochhourn and not a fast road. It is very beautiful along by Lochs Garry and Quoich so enjoy it but leave time for the walk. The descent to Kinlochhourn is steep and full of sharp bends.

Barrisdale was once a thriving centre of population; the glen is wide and fertile and the sheltered bay provided a good anchorage. It is said that as many as 50 fishing boats used to anchor there. But disaster struck in the shape of the potato blight in 1846, and then the herring failed. Knoydart belonged to the MacDonells of Glengarry. The 16th chief died in 1852, leaving an impoverished people. His widow Josephine 'cleared' the remaining people to

Barrisdale Bay and Ladhar Bheinn

make way for sheep, before selling the land to a lowland ironmaster. Today there is one farm at Barrisdale, and occasional yachts anchor in the bay.

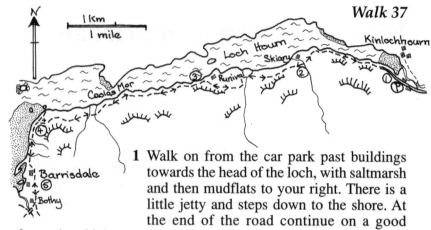

Walk 37

1 Walk on from the car park past buildings towards the head of the loch, with saltmarsh and then mudflats to your right. There is a little jetty and steps down to the shore. At the end of the road continue on a good footpath, which rounds a rocky bluff and skirts the steep hillside just above the water. The loch here is very narrow and hemmed in by steep slopes on either side. As you walk on the loch gradually becomes wider, the slope on your left recedes a little and round a corner you reach the settlement of Skiary, only accessible on foot or by boat. This was 'cleared', but one house is still inhabited.

2 Cross the burn on a bridge and tackle the first of three uphill stretches. Go through a gap in a fence near the top, cross a boggy area and enjoy the view along the loch. Descend to a pebbly bay and then almost immediately start to go uphill again. This climb takes you up to a col, where pine and birch trees adorn the hillside. There is a crag, Creag Raonabhal, to your right, and the path winds down by a burn, then crosses two more, to return to the shore beyond the croft of Runival.

3 Now for about 1 ½ miles / 2 ½ km the path keeps just above the shore, winding through splendid pine and birch trees at the foot of the steep hillside. Anywhere along here you might see an otter or a seal, and terns fly up the loch to fish in spring and summer. Look up at the skyline too, because this is golden eagle country. A wooded promontory from the far side almost divides the loch in two at the narrows, Caolas Mor. Go over another footbridge over a tumbling burn, the Allt a'Chaolas Bhig, and then climb again, more gently

142

this time, to contour round the hillside well above the shore. Come round a corner and go down a steep valley to the shore of Barrisdale Bay, by the ruins of a church.

4 A track runs along above the shore. You have a choice here, either to turn right and walk down to the tidal islet Fraoch Eilean, where boats land bringing people across from Arnisdale further down the loch, or to turn left and walk on up into the glen. Maybe you would like to do both. Across the bay and ahead of you as you walk along the shore towards the glen is Ladhar Bheinn, pronounced Larven, one of the most magnificent Munros, seen from its best side here. As the track curves into the glen more mountains appear, notably Luinne Bheinn at the head and, looking back across Barrisdale Bay and Loch Hourn, Beinn Sgritheall towers above the tiny row of cottages at Arnisdale. Barrisdale is fertile and welcoming. There is a house behind a hedge, surrounded by trees, and a farm, and a bothy.

5 In summer there may be tents beyond the bothy. But unless you intend to stay, leave time for the long return walk to Kinlochhourn—still another 7 miles / 11.4km, and the up-hills are just as high and steep as they were on the way out.

Otters

Practicals

Type of walk: This must come high on the list of best low-level walks in Scotland. It is remote and takes you into country otherwise difficult of access. The path is good, but not flat. The views are superb.

Distance: 14 miles / 23km
Time: An all day walk
Maps: OS Explorer 413 and 414 / Landranger 33

38

Loch Lundie

Park in the large parking area beside Glengarry post office, grid ref. 302010. To access this leave the A82 at the sign for the Glengarry Hotel and Kyle of Lochalsh and drive along the A87 for a mile to where the parking lies to your left.

After Culloden, the clan chiefs became landlords, rather than guardians of their people, seeking higher rents, which the poor lands could not provide. Later they leased huge grazings to sheep farmers. Hundreds of the Clan MacDonell chose, or were forced, to emigrate in the late 1700s and early 1800s. Glengarry county in Ohio owes its name to the indomitable people of the glen who found their early days there as full of hardships as they did here.

Loch Lundie and Ben Tee

1 Walk on along the A87, remaining on the same side of the road, for just under ¼ mile / ½ km. Then cross the A-road just beyond the bridge over the Aldernaig Burn and walk ahead. In a few steps bear right up a well made track between two cottages to a gate, with several notices on it. Beyond, walk an idyllic track through fine deciduous woodland, with the burn beside you, through trees. Here you might spot red squirrels. Pass through a deer gate. In the

birch woodland, at the right **Walk 38**
time of the year, thrive the
bright red and white fly
agaric toadstools. Then the
track continues a little more
steeply and roughly before it
levels, and has heather
growing along the middle.

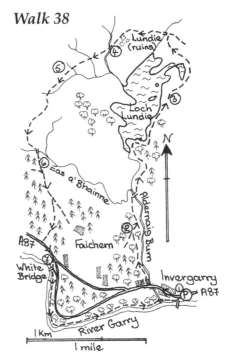

2 At the T-junction of tracks,
turn right onto a level track.
This passes through more
pleasing birch woodland and
then conifers where you
might see, in the tops of the
trees, a flock of crossbills
and mixed tits. Cross a
vehicle bridge over the burn
and carry on through birch.
Then the way emerges from
the trees and crosses a small
area of open moor with a
weir, to the left, on the
Aldernaig. Carry on through more birch to come to a ladderstile in
a deer fence. If you stand on the top you can see Beinn Tee,
dominating the glen and the other mountains. Once over, the track
continues through scattered Scots pine and the burn is wide and
sluggish. Follow the track as it winds on until you have your first

Crossbill

145

glimpse of Loch Lundie, a pretty sheet of water with several fascinating islands, one of which is circular with a solitary yew tree. Go on past a boat house and a small jetty.

3 Climb the next ladderstile over a deer fence and walk on into heather moorland. Follow the track as it eventually begins to wind well above the head of the loch, always with Beinn Tee overlooking the lovely pool. Carry on until you reach a T-junction of tracks, where you turn left. Cross a plank bridge and go on along the grassy way. Soon you can see the boathouse across Loch Lundie. As you pass under Creagan Lundie, on the right, look left to see stone foundations and low walls, all that remains of the village of Lundie, and imagine the hard life of the inhabitants.

4 The track then brings you to a ford over a shallow burn, which flows through a very wide shingle bed. It is generally easy to cross but might present problems when in spate. Go on ahead to the next burn crossed by the remnants of a timber bridge. It is quite unsafe; you should cross on stones. At the third burn the bridge has more timbers but demands a balancing act to cross and you may prefer, again, to cross on stones. If the last three burns prove impossible to cross, return by the same route to the parking area. This walk carries on to come to two deer gates, both padlocked. To the right of the right-hand gate is a stile over the barbed wire fence. Continue on along a better track gently climbing over the heather moorland, with just the occasional boggy patch.

5 Cross a stream on two firm planks and go on to ascend, quite steeply, a rough path, which after rain becomes a stream. At the top, bear slightly left to reach the brow, where you will want to pause to enjoy the superb view of the mountains soaring above the forest. Then begin your descent. When you reach a very wet area go left, where other walkers have made their way, and then gradually return to the main path again. Follow the distinct path as it bends a little left and descends slightly as it crosses the moorland, with one or two boggy patches to negotiate. This brings you close, on the right, to the corner of a deer fence. Cross a fine wooden bridge over the Eas a'Bhainne. Carry on, with the deer fence to your right, to go through a large kissing gate in more deer fencing. Walk ahead along a grassy track, with a boundary fence to the left and the plantation to your right.

6 Join a forest track and walk ahead (ignoring the right turn). Continue

146

until the track divides. Take the right branch and go on descending the easy-to-walk track, with another superb view of Beinn Tee as you drop down this pleasing corridor through trees. Just before you join the A87, move left to pass through a gap to the side of the padlocked deer gates. Cross the road and walk left along the grassy verge for 300 yds / 274m. Just after the signpost for Faichem, take a path, down right, to reach a narrow road. To the right is the White Bridge over the River Garry. Do not cross but you might want to enjoy the fine view from it of the cascades on the wide river.

7 Return from the bridge and turn into the signposted riverside path to Invergarry. This takes you on a good safe path, high above the river, passing through lush vegetation, where chickweed wintergreen grows, and forest trees. After passing more cascades and braiding, the path drops down closer to the stately river. Look for goosanders and dippers on the hurrying water. Stroll on to cross two fine wooden bridges and, eventually, to arrive at an iron bridge (Black Bridge) over the river. Here turn left, away from the bridge, and climb several steps to reach the parking area by Glengarry post office.

Chickweed
Wintergreen

cHl

Practicals

Type of walk: A very pleasing walk through contrasting environments.

Distance: 7 ½ miles / 12km
Time: 4 hours
Maps: OS Explorer 400 / Landranger 34

39

Bridge of Oich, Fort Augustus, Inchnacardoch Forest

Park at Oich Bridge parking area, grid ref. 339036. See walk 33 for access.

The **Caledonian Canal** that links the Moray Firth, Loch Ness, Loch Oich, Loch Lochy and Loch Linnhe was completed in 1822 after 19 years of work. It was constructed by **Thomas Telford** who met tremendous difficulties due to the porosity of the ground and differences in levels between lochs. This problem was overcome by building 29 locks. The construction cost about £1,300,000, funded by the Treasury partly to provide employment and also to provide a sheltered route for naval vessels, prone to attack by French

Kytra Lock

vessels, while they voyaged around the stormy north coast of Scotland.

Fort Augustus is located at the southern end of Loch Ness. After the Jacobite uprising of 1715 and 1719, General Wade was appointed as commander of the forces in northern Britain. His task was to restore order in the Highlands. At that time there were no roads in the Highlands, north of Dunkeld. Also there was a great need to improve communications between the military posts. Between 1725 and 1733 his troops built 400km of hard road and 40 bridges to link the barracks at Fort William, Fort Augustus, Inverness and Ruthven. The first barracks were built in the grounds of the Lovat Arms Hotel. Wade had doubts about its suitability and a much larger fort—Fort Augustus—was built near the Loch side.

Walk 39

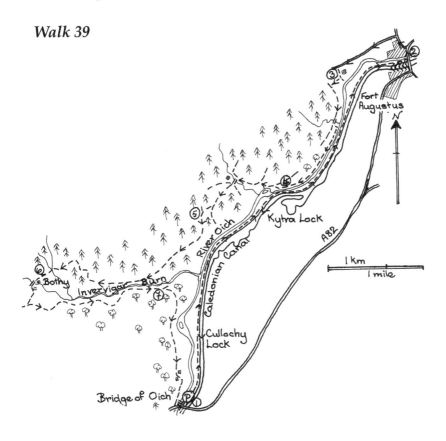

1 From the car park, join the towpath, part of the Great Glen Way and walk with the canal to your right. Soon the canal comes close to the River Oich, which runs parallel with, but lower than, the canal. Cross the wide cobbled overflow where excess water in the canal runs off into the river. Go past Cullochy lock and walk the pleasing way, with woodland on both sides of the waterway. Cross another canal overflow and then pass the attractive lock at Kytra. Beyond, the canal becomes very wide. The next overflow you reach is controlled by a huge pipe, where water passes below the towpath and then tumbles down a stone ladder into the river. Stroll on into Fort Augustus where you pass a flight of five locks, which takes boats an hour to negotiate. Walk on to join the road.

2 Turn left and pause on the bridge over the River Oich. Look right to see the ruined bridge, a temporary timber structure, used after the stone bridge, carrying traffic into the village, was swept away in 1849. To the left stands, in the river, the remaining pillar of the railway viaduct. Go on past the supermarket, the information centre and a car park. Walk on a little way until you can see a signed left turn for 'Forest Walks and River Oich Walk'. Climb a railed slope onto the road above and turn left. Follow the road as it winds right and comes to a T-junction where you turn left. Carry on along the pleasing way and follow it as it winds sharp left and begins to descend under some splendid beech. Stroll on until you come to the Forestry Office.

3 Walk left, beyond the building, and continue where the way becomes a track. Just before a car park, take a way-marked right turn to pass through a gate to walk across a pasture. Here many young oak trees thrive. At a T-junction of tracks, turn left and stride the pleasant track as it winds right, soon to cross a burn by a stone bridge. A few steps beyond, take an unsigned narrow path going off left. This descends, delightfully, through birch woodland to come to a wide track, where you turn right. The pine needle-carpeted way leads you, for just over a mile, through mixed woodland, close to the River Oich.

4 On reaching some extensive rapids on the Oich where your progress is barred by vegetation, leave the river and move right on a narrow path, through the woodland, to join a forest track. Turn left and walk on, ignoring the next right turn. Carry on to pass through a gate and keep to the right of a small forest car park. Stroll on until you can see a way-out sign where you turn left and cross a bridge over a burn. Here take the second left, a signed footpath that climbs through a lovely corridor in the forest at the foot of Torr Dhuin. Continue ascending gently for just over a ¼ mile / 0.5km and then turn right, to descend a track to join a forest road, where you turn left.

5 Walk on the very pleasant way for about 2 ¼ miles / 3.5km, through mixed woodland, coming close to the Invervigar Burn (heard but not seen) before climbing steadily to where the trees have been clear-felled and the track ends. Here bear slightly left to pick up a narrow, rough, stalker's path that brings you to the side of a shallow burn. Step across on convenient stones but, if in spate, you may have to wade. Walk on along the side of another narrow burn, on the stony track. This leads to a deer gate which you push open.

6 Beyond, follow the 'New Path' sign through scattered trees and bushes to come round the bothy to the side of the Allt Dail a' Chuirn, which you cross on a flat wooden footbridge. Go on along a grassy path to pass a cottage, now a byre, which is losing its slates. From the front of this building, continue on a grassy trod for a short distance to come to a wide landrover track, where you turn left. Walk on along the track as it crosses high moorland, with scattered mature birch, to go over a bridge. Carry on as the track starts to descend, keeping parallel with the Invervigar Burn, which gathers water from many other tributaries as it tumbles through its delectable tree-lined ravine.

Red Squirrel

151

7 Eventually you arrive at a Y-junction of tracks. Ignore the left turn and carry on ahead. As you descend the attractive way, you can see the Oich Bridge just below. Go on down and down. Ignore the left turn to the fine cantilever bridge and go on to wind round a huge crag, topped with trees, where you might spot a red squirrel. Bear left to come to a gate on to the A82. Turn left to return to the parking area by the canal.

Wood anemones

Practicals

Type of walk: A long pleasing walk by a canal, alongside a river, through forestry and over moorland. Some people will find fording the burn, up on the moor, difficult when in spate. Choose a good day after a dry spell or several days after heavy rain has ceased.

Distance:	14 miles / 23km
Time:	7 hours
Maps:	OS Explorer 400 / Landranger 34

NB: If ever the bridge over the Invervigar Burn is rebuilt the walk would be shortened by 3 $^{1}/_{3}$ miles / 5.3km

40

Fort Augustus,
Corrieyairack Pass, Culachy

Park at the burial ground, grid ref. 378080. This is accessed from
Fort Augustus by driving south-west along the A82 for just over ½
mile / 1km. Here turn left, opposite a caravan and camping site,
signposted Kilchuiman (Kilchumein) burial ground. If the few
spaces outside the wall of the burial ground are full you may have
to park in Fort Augustus and follow the route from there.

The Great Glen slices Scotland in two from Inverness to Fort
William. Glaciers sheared along an underlying fault line during
the Ice Age to carve out the U-shaped valley that today contains
Loch Ness, Loch Oich, Loch Lochy and Loch Linnhe. The Great

Culachy House

Glen formed an ancient travelling route across Scotland. Today people still travel along it by boat on the Caledonian Canal, on foot by The Great Glen Way, on bicycle by the Great Glen Cycle route or by car on the A82. The 73 mile / 117km long distance footpath, the Great Glen Way, opened in April 2002. It links the Atlantic Ocean in the west with the North Sea in the east.

The track over the **Corrieyairack Pass** is a General Wade road. It linked Fort Augustus with Laggan in Speyside. Wade is reputed to have said that it was 'as easy and practicable for wheeled carriages as any other road in the country'. Alas some carriages were blown over. There are dramatic accounts of civilians perishing in blizzards and soldiers succumbing to the cold, having over-refreshed themselves with whisky. The road was often blocked by snow for several months during the winter and sometimes bodies were retrieved only after the spring thaw.

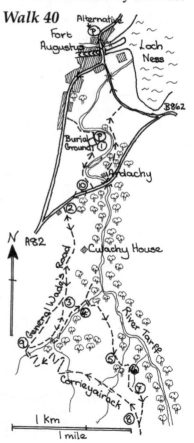

Walk 40

1 From the parking area, climb the steps into the burial ground where you should pause to view the historic graves. Walk ahead and then bear left to climb a stone stile over the wall, on the right, onto a good track. Continue on along the tree-shaded way, with open views to the right across the Glen to Beinn Tee. To your left the River Tarff flows noisily through its very deep wooded ravine. At the track end, turn left and then immediately right to join the quiet Ardachy Road. Turn right, following a sign 'To the Corrieyairack Pass', going by the striking entrance gates to Culachy House. After ¼ mile / ½ km, and just before a house on the left, take a grassy trod, signed Corrieyairack Pass.

2 Climb the short grassy way to pass through a gate onto General Wade's Military Road, now a scheduled monument. Soon the trod joins a smoother track coming up from an unusual bridge. Continue uphill to pass, on the left, the magnificent Culachy House, with its crenellations, crow steppings and turrets. Beyond the house are some birches and on some of these you might spot a tree creeper. Then the way becomes much rougher underfoot. Go through a gate in the deer fence and climb the track through open heather moorland until you reach a point where the power lines cross overhead.

3 Leave the track, left, on a thin path and slant right to join a wide pleasing grassy terrace-like trod and follow it as it winds right round a hillock. Carry on parallel with a deer fence that runs down to your left. When you can see where the fence turns left, leave the

track on a narrow path that drops down through heather to the fence corner and then slants on down to the side of the Connache burn, a tributary of the Tarff. Pass through birch and cross a flat concrete bridge over the burn. Wind left to cross a plank footbridge over a tiny stream and walk downstream through rowan and birch to pass through a kissing gate in a deer fence. The grassy track continues through this charming valley. Cross the burn on another concrete bridge and walk on. As you go look for dippers hunting for prey in the shallow cascades.

4 Watch out for the first sighting of a stone bridge over the burn. Walk on a few steps to take an acute right turn that leads down to the bridge, which you cross. Then climb the continuing track, through birch, to emerge from the trees high above the Tarff valley with glorious views ahead. Follow the track that keeps to the rim of the hillside. Pause here to look back to Fort Augustus, Loch Ness and the mountains beyond. In late summer the lovely grass of Parnassus adorns the way. The high level way contours on most pleasantly with high hills all about.

Grass of Parnassus

155

Soon you can see the huge craggy sides of a gorge through which flows the Tarff.

5 As you near birch woodland the now indistinct track divides. Keep to the lower one to come to the side of a narrow crevice through which flows the Allt Ceum na Goibhire. Drop down a short steep slope to step across the little stream below a waterfall. Then climb up an equally steep slope to continue on the track. Go on along the grassy way, with care, as it winds round the edge of a steep slope on a narrow path. Cross a small pebbly washout and then go along another short stretch of narrow path. The way then carries on as a wide terraced path. From here you can see Culachy House far down the glen. Go through an ancient gate.

6 Here turn right and climb up steeply, keeping parallel with the fence, on your right, to come to another gate. Turn left and cross the rough pasture to arrive at the edge of a wooded hollow. Do not continue (because of another washout) but turn right and ascend the clear small path that climbs steeply upwards, soon to join a transverse path above the gully. Turn left and follow this to a deer gate onto heather moorland.

7 Beyond walk a path that keeps parallel with the deer fence on your left, first avoiding a largish boggy patch. Where the fence turns down left, carry on along a pleasing green path to cross a small stream. Then follow the good path over the moor. Enjoy this airy way where you may spot black grouse. After a delightful stroll you arrive, suddenly, at the Corrieyairack Pass road, where you turn right.

8 Follow the track for nearly a mile, passing through a gate where you should notice a short stretch of ancient cobbling. Then the

Black grouse

156

track descends the sleep slopes towards the Connachie Burn in a series of wide zig-zags, roughly surfaced and hard on your booted feet! Each turn brings another superb view, in the distance, of at least twelve fine mountains. As you go look for roe deer moving through the bracken.

9 At the valley bottom, step across the Connachie Burn and turn right onto a fine grassy trod, part of which you walked earlier. Carry on gently climbing and follow the way as it winds round a hillock and then becomes an almost indistinct path, winding left, parallel with the power lines, to come to the track over the Pass once more. Turn right and continue through the deer gate. Go on past Culachy House. Leave the track where it swings right to the unusual stone bridge. Walk on down to pass through the gate and descend the grassy trod to the narrow road.

10 Walk right for ¼ mile / ½ km, turn left and then immediately left again, to walk the track to the burial ground and the parking area.

Practicals

Type of walk: A lovely walk through delightful countryside.

Distance: 7 ½ miles / 12km
Time: 4 hours
Maps: OS Explorer 401 / Landranger 34

NB If you have had to park in Fort Augustus and would like an alternative return route, do not turn left from the Ardachy Road but continue on along the road to cross the Ardachy Bridge over the Tarff. Turn left just beyond the bridge, signed 'Ness Viewpoint' and go down a track to Ardachy. Bear right, signed with a discreet white arrow on a post. Follow the pleasant track through woodland then with a fenced field to the right and a wooded bank to the left and the Tarff below. The path descends gently through trees to reach the B862. Turn left to walk into the village. On reaching the A82 turn right to the car park.

Clan Walks

A series of walks described by Mary Welsh, covering some of the most popular holiday areas in the Scottish Highlands and Islands.

Titles published so far include:

1. 44 WALKS ON THE ISLE OF ARRAN
2. WALKING THE ISLE OF SKYE
3. WALKING WESTER ROSS
4. WALKS IN PERTHSHIRE
5. WALKING THE WESTERN ISLES
6. WALKING ORKNEY
7. WALKING SHETLAND
8. WALKING THE ISLES OF ISLAY, JURA AND COLONSAY
9. WALKS ON CANNA, RUM, EIGG AND MUCK
10. WALKS ON TIREE, COLL, COLONSAY AND A TASTE OF MULL
11. WALKING DUMFRIES AND GALLOWAY
12. WALKING ARGYLL AND BUTE
13. WALKING DEESIDE, DONSIDE AND ANGUS
14. WALKING THE TROSSACHS, LOCH LOMONDSIDE AND THE CAMPSIE FELLS
15. WALKING GLENCOE, LOCHABER AND THE GREAT GLEN

OTHER TITLES IN PREPARATION

Books in this series can be ordered through booksellers anywhere. In the event of difficulty write to Clan Books, The Cross, DOUNE, FK16 6BE, Scotland.